WHAT AN EXPERIENCE!

To Fran and Mel,

Enjoy glimpses into
my twelve amazing and
happy years as a
Volunteer.

With love,

Rowena

x

2022,

WHAT AN EXPERIENCE!

IVER NATURE STUDY CENTRE

SALLY MUNN

Matador
Unit E2 Airfield Business Park,
Harrison Road, Market Harborough,
Leicestershire. LE16 7UL
Tel: 0116 279 2299
Email: books@troubador.co.uk
Web: www.troubador.co.uk/matador
Twitter: @matadorbooks

ISBN 978 180313 181 8

British Library Cataloguing in Publication Data.
A catalogue record for this book is available from the British Library.

Printed and bound by CPI Group (UK) Ltd, Croydon, CR0 4YY
Typeset in 11pt Minion Pro by Troubador Publishing Ltd, Leicester, UK

Matador is an imprint of Troubador Publishing Ltd

Everything which was achieved at Iver Nature Study Centre would not have been possible without the extraordinary array of talents, goodwill and hard work provided by the volunteers. To each and every one of them, I dedicate this book.

FOREWORD

What was it about Iver Nature Study Centre which made it so special? After all, there were hundreds of environmental centres dotted all over the country. Roger Ferrin wrote in my retirement card, 'I look forward to reading your book'. I knew what he meant because he had been pestering me (in the nicest sense) to write about the true Iver. There was something about this particular Centre which was unique and, every time I saw Roger, usually on Tuesday mornings when depositing his daughters from the car, he would say, "Have you started the book yet?"

I retired from the Centre in 2009 but, despite having made a start not long afterwards, only now have had both the time and opportunity to tell the full story of a wonderful place which made people give of themselves so readily, so generously and in such extraordinary ways.

Finally, I have written my story and achieved my goal. I hope you enjoy the journey.

Sally Munn
2021

CONTENTS

ONE
1991
IN THE BEGINNING

IVER NATURE STUDY CENTRE'S BACKGROUND.
ACTIVITIES OFFERED DURING THE EARLY YEARS.
OUR INITIAL EDUCATION PACKAGES.

Iver Nature Study Centre's background

To start at the beginning…

Iver Nature Study Centre (INSC), Buckinghamshire, was the brainchild of one, Wendy Varcoe, who worked for the Denham-based environmental charity, Groundwork Colne Valley (GWCV), now called Groundwork South. Her idea was to create a place where special needs people could enjoy the countryside and observe nature in a safe environment.

National Grid, then known as the Central Electricity Generating Board (CEGB), owned a two-acre piece of land which lay between their substation and Mansfield Farm. The site, once the home of Mansfield House, had become derelict by the time they took it over, with their intention to use it as offices. However, the condition of the building did not make this feasible.

I believe it took two years to gain the necessary planning permission, re-landscape the area and put in a visitors' cabin. On 21 September 1990, local residents, the esteemed actor, Sir John Mills CBE and his playwright wife, Lady Mills (Mary Hayley Bell) did the honours and declared Iver Nature Study Centre open.

Meanwhile, I was living in Pinner, Middlesex with my husband and two small boys and decided I would like to become an environmental volunteer. I drove to Denham Country Park where I met Geraldine (Gerry) Alexander in the publicity department of Groundwork and, following an informal chat, became an official volunteer. One of my first duties was to interview the Project Officer who was running Iver Nature Study Centre, then write a piece to publicise the place.

I went along for my first site visit and was shown the visitors' cabin, small meadow, 'The Secret Garden', ponds and the rest of the grounds. As I looked around, my immediate thought was, 'what a fabulous place'. My mind was racing with what I could do with it. Anyway, I wrote the piece, thought nothing more of it, until the telephone rang one day. It was the lovely Judith Hammond, Office Manager for GWCV.

"Why don't you apply for the job?" she asked.

"What job?"

"Project Officer at INSC. The current one is leaving to go back to Scotland."

A few years later Judith, after leaving the Denham office, became one of the four secretaries I had the pleasure to work with in the Study Centre's office over the years. Each is detailed in The Ladies in the Office in the next chapter.

Although the advert in the local press stated they wanted a graduate, I was offered an interview, despite having no degree. In fact, I had left school when I was seventeen years old, having scraped though five 'O' levels and realised, in no way was I 'A' level material. It was my first interview in over a decade and I was astonished to be offered the job, but reluctantly had to turn it down on being told it had gone from part-time to full-time. I did not want my boys to be latchkey children. About a week later, they called me back to the Centre and asked if I would consider running the place part-time until they could re-advertise in the national press. Yes, I would, as I wanted the job so much.

When I arrived home that afternoon, a freebie magazine had been delivered. I pondered, opened it at the agencies page then dialled one of the numbers.

"I don't suppose you have someone who could come between 3.30pm and 6 on weekdays to look after two delightful boys?"

"Yes, we do," came the reply. "A grandmother has recently come on the books …"

Ironically, it transpired I had met this lady a few months before, at a local county hockey trial. She was there with her grandson and I with my elder boy and we had spent the whole afternoon discussing the state of education!

I telephoned Groundwork. "Can I change my mind?"

I became Manager of INSC on 13 January 1991 and stayed for eighteen wonderful years which changed my life.

*

My first day.

I remember opening the gates, unlocking the cabin door, dumping my bag in the tiny room which served as an office then walking around the site and thinking, 'what have I done?' The task ahead of me was enormous, and there was only me to do it. The one thing I knew was that I had to make things exciting. I did not want just another environmental study centre where people wandered around, not taking anything in. As a friend advised, "Give them something interesting and the rest will follow."

I had been at the Centre for about a fortnight when I arrived one morning to find the inclement weather had caused a burst water-pipe. The cost of repair was rather high which did not endear me to the powers that be but I did explain the outside pipe would have been better lagged. Not an auspicious start.

Around the same time as this incident, a tall, stick-thin gentleman arrived at the Centre and asked what it was all about. I flustered the answers. I was on my own, trying to get my head round how to sort the garden, keep the cabin clean and tidy, devise activities, seek sponsorship and get the place publicised.

His name was Keith Macqueen and he became my very first volunteer, staying for ten years until he and his wife Jean, moved away from the area. Every Tuesday he would come and find me to ask what needed doing. He became known as 'Keith, if you have a moment …' as I would invariably reply, "Keith, if you have a moment, would you …cut down, screw back, paint, maintain …" He also did many other things I had not asked him to do but which he saw needed attention. He was capable, reliable and practical. He never complained and just got on with everything which needed doing.

As the weeks went by, I made contact with local organisations which might be able to help us with sponsorship or gifts in kind and also began to devise activities which would draw people in. Originally, the Centre was developed purely for special needs people but, three months into my tenure, a lady came to see what we offered then said she thought it was prejudiced and should be for everyone. From then on, I advertised the Centre as a place where 'individuals and community groups, irrespective of age, ability or background, can come and take part in activities which have an educational, environmental and/or therapeutic theme to them.'

Wanting to devise activities which would encourage people of all ages and abilities to visit the Centre more than once or twice, I decided to break the year up into four quarters. I then planned days and special weeks with hands-on activities. Whenever possible, I would bring in people who could demonstrate a skill, or were specialists in their field, for those particular themes. For example, during Barn Owl Week, we had a representative from the Hawk and Owl

Trust who brought a beautiful example of this bird. During Arts and Crafts Week, we covered topics such as wood carving, ceramics, pottery, corn dollies and cross-stitching, to name but a few. Volunteers, husband and wife, Vic and Jan Merrill managed to find a hedgehog during that special week and I provided a chocolate sponge cake in the shape of the delightful creature.

*

In early 2021, having settled into my latest home, after retrieving the many boxes from storage and friends' attics, I set about unpacking each. Those marked 'INSC' were given the highest priority and, among the initial ones opened was a copy of the report I had been asked to write about the first year of the Study Centre, some of which I would like to share with you because it will give you a better understanding of our aims and achievements in those early months. The following is taken from that 1992 report, written eight months after I started the first of what were to become eighteen years at Iver.

…I am pleased to say over two thousand people have sampled its facilities, in a surprisingly varying capacity.

Those who visit the site, some of whom have a disability, come into one of three categories: workers, visiting groups and activists.

Workers vary from two to four groups who come each week and help in the garden, mostly with weeding, clearing and digging.

Visiting groups are those who have come to the Centre for an outing. They spend between two and three hours enjoying the sights and sounds of Iver and either stay to lunch, which they bring, or to afternoon tea which I tend to provide.

Activists are groups who regularly take part in the planned special weeks, where all activities are geared to a particular natural history topic. For example: frogs, barn owls, arts and crafts, the 'I Spy Nature Trail', 'The Countryside Game' and the drama sessions. These have all proved very popular, as participants learn through games, touch, co-ordination, control, smell, sight etc. about their natural environment.

Over these months, I have received a vast amount of help from volunteers, whether it be Keith, who comes in once a week to carry out essential maintenance, Matthew and Andrew, who are doing community service for their Duke of Edinburgh Award, Ian with his lawn mower or Kerstin, from Germany, who volunteers every day. We are fortunate to have various able-bodied groups of school children who also wish to help in a variety of ways.

Many of those who take part in activities at Iver have one or more disabilities. They include the blind or partially sighted, stroke sufferers, those living with Alzheimer's disease and some who are enduring the agony of loneliness. There is obviously a need for safe places, such as Iver Nature Study Centre, because our clients have come from Buckinghamshire, Hillingdon, Berkshire, Kent, Hertfordshire, Surrey, Sussex and some Greater London boroughs …

Activities offered during the early years

The first activity we offered was 'Frog Week'. For this, I created some visual displays and kept the actual teaching contents simple. I remember hunting for frogspawn but soon, members of the public were telephoning, wanting to off-load spawn they found in their pond and occasionally, the actual frogs themselves. During the first year, we did not have any trouble showing visitors the real thing. I recall keeping some frogspawn in a container, successfully rearing the froglets which a children's group then released into the big pond at the appropriate time.

What was interesting to note over the years was, in the beginning, plenty of frogspawn was laid and developed normally. However, as time went by, it was getting harder and harder to find any, and the clumps we found would develop from the egg stage into tadpoles but not into froglets. By the time I left, in 2009, there was very little spawn and not even the eggs were hatching.

We eventually got 'Frog Week' down to a fine art. Those participating would be shown a pond habitat and, if possible, find spawn, then be talked through a paste-and-stick activity, showing the life cycle of this amphibian. Next, with a small, plastic flower pot for its body, using pre-cut shapes and glue, each person would create their own frog by gluing on a green face, black eyes, a yellow smile, long green arms, hands, concertinaed legs and webbed feet. Over the years, we must have cut out and made many hundreds.

I also obtained a game called 'Hop in the Pot', whereby the players flicked plastic frogs into a little container.

It was a very good way for participants of all ages and abilities to improve their co-ordination and often caused lots of laughter.

*

The first project I undertook was to create an outdoor game in an area both entered and exited from the pathway running alongside the big pond. Here, adults and children of all ages, with or without special needs who, for whatever reason, were unable to access the countryside easily, could have fun while learning about the natural world.

After the design, which I called 'The Countryside Game', became a reality, pupils from Iver Heath County First School helped with planting flowers along the wide, paved, 'U'-shaped path, stocking the mini-pond and devising some of the questions for the game I had envisioned. Played along the lines of Ludo, each participant, in turn, threw a large sponge dice. The paving stones were numbered in sequence and, after the question for that particular number was answered correctly, the player moved forward two spaces. Incorrectly answered meant moving back two spaces. The questions were relatively easy, varying from the spoken word, using the identification boards along the side of the footpath, to searching for clues under a log pile or in the middle of a mound of fallen leaves. This encouraged those taking part to learn a little more about the countryside. It also promoted reading skills, working together, communication, figure work and, most of all, enjoyment.

Sally Magnusson officially opened 'The Countryside Game' in May then, in October that year, for the part they had played in creating the game, the Iver Heath pupils won a bronze award at the Royal Anniversary Trust Awards.

Our initial education packages

As we progressed, we offered various activity packages relating to the natural world which included: 'The Environment', 'Feed the Birds Fortnight', 'Sea and Seashore', 'Apple Fortnight' and 'The Science of Christmas', all of which were adapted to the age and ability of the participants. It was not long before local junior schools i.e. children aged five to eleven, began booking by class, when the children were learning about a particular project. There were frequent weeks when we seemed to have a school every day.

Every package had its own worksheets but the emphasis was on each participant looking and seeing how nature worked and, in most activities, it was essential to include an art and craft session so everyone could use a cross-section of skills whilst learning and enjoying themselves. I wanted all those who took part to experience working both on their own and as a group, using various skills such as observation, verbal reasoning, dexterity, reading, writing and arithmetic.

For some of the hands-on stick-and-paste activities, as well as glue, paints, colouring pencils etc, if appropriate for the scene, pots of coloured glitter were put on the tables. We soon realised this was a mistake after several children overenthusiastically covered most of their creation with it. It was a nightmare to sweep up afterwards as it went everywhere, and we often went home with sparkly clothes, hair and face. From then on, the large containers were kept out of reach and only a small amount, in a tube or saucer, was given to those who asked.

On one memorable occasion, a seven-year-old asked his mother for glitter. She replied, "Ask the lie-die (i.e. myself) fo' a glit'a."

From that day, my initial school group volunteers ribbed me, referring to me as 'the lie-die wif a glit'a'! Fun days – or should that be 'fun dies'?

*

As well as education packages, over the course of the next few years, we offered birthday parties, mainly run by Jill Nicholas who was brilliant at devising different nature themes. We also had an after-school nature club, pre-school nature play sessions and started holiday activities which we called 'I'm Bored'. We set up a Saturday morning gardening session for children then, for nearly five years, ran a Saturday morning group for reluctant readers which we called 'Once upon a Time'. More about those later.

Two education packages proved to be staggeringly successful: 'The Environment' and 'The Science of Christmas', with schools coming back year after year to take part. Our aim was not to confuse the children with facts but simply make them aware of their surroundings by encouraging them to observe their environment in more detail and to question things.

Once the schools started to book for our education packages, we had to bring some semblance of order to how things were to be run since, as a rule, classes would consist of up to thirty-five children. Eventually, a fifty-by-thirty foot marquee was purchased then erected in the car park from spring until autumn. When the children arrived, we would collect their lunchboxes and, to keep them safe and out of the way, put these in a large rubbish bin, much to the amusement of the children! We all went into the marquee where the children sat and listened to 'the riot act' which was kept simple. 'Do not run. Do not wander off. Do let an adult know if you require the toilet'. Too many rules and regulations would have spoiled their enjoyment.

For 'The Environment' package, the class was split into three groups and, throughout the day, would have forty minutes to explore each of three specific habitats: pond, meadow and woodland. There were simple worksheets covering each subject to complete during their visit.

For the pond activity, the children visited three, each of which differed from the others in both size and habitat. These were: the purpose-built, raised pond in front of the visitors' cabin, the large pond surrounded by trees and crossed by means of a wooden bridge and thirdly, a small, sunken pond in 'The Secret Garden'. This last pond was in a sheltered area, hidden behind high stone walls, with entry gained through an old, wooden door.

We did not allow the children to pond dip, mainly because of the time factor but also the sheer number of children would have ruined the pond habitats. Instead, we filled enamel trays with pond life from each of the three, ready for them to observe with eyes or magnifying glass then talk about the different creatures and how they moved. The leader, either an Iver volunteer who was part of the education

Pond Dipping Investigations
©Kareth Paterson

team or myself, would fill in details of which part of the pond each inhabited, what was top predator and so on.

Once, when I was running this session, two boys, wearing football shirts, were mucking about, not taking a blind bit of notice of what was going on. I called them over, pointed to the tray of pond creatures and said, "What position would you put these creatures in, if they were part of a football team?"

Their reaction was quizzical but one of sudden interest.

"See this one," I said, pointing to a whirligig beetle, circling its way around the enamel tray. "I'd have him as a midfielder because he's quick and all over the place. Look at the creatures and watch how they are moving then try and identify them from the charts and see if you can form a team." A short while later, when quietly checking them, they were still hunched over the tray discussing tactics.

The meadow activity, the one I loved to do, began with me standing by the closed gate, chatting with the children to establish exactly what a meadow consisted of. In ours, to make it more interesting, we had planted a mini-orchard as well. Like the pond worksheet, the meadow lesson also had three parts to it. Firstly, having walked to the centre of the meadow, the group was asked to lie on the grass, close their eyes, listen to the various sounds then decide which were man-made and which were nature at work. After five minutes, when asked what they had heard, the children invariably said first, the calling of the birds, surprisingly over the hum of the wires from the National Grid and from the whooshing sound of vehicles on the M25, often thought to be the sound of a waterfall.

In the early days, we had no trouble getting the children to lie on the grass and close their eyes. By the time I left, the children would remain standing, shuffling around, only for a minute or so as, when initially asked to lie down, their response was invariably, "Oh, it's dirty. I can't do that."

Next, the children were paired off, told to search for minibeasts then draw one in the appropriate box on their worksheet. Finally, they were asked to choose a flower growing in the meadow, draw it as accurately as possible then answer the questions at the foot of the page. These were worded in such a way that the children had to really look at the whole plant to answer the questions which included: 'How are the leaves arranged on the stem – opposite or alternate?' 'Where are they positioned – at the bottom or along the stem?' 'Where on the stem are the buds and the flowers?' There were drawings alongside

Dear all at liver nature centre.
   All of beech class had a relly good time.
   It was proaply the best school trip ever.
   Thank you so much, for shearing the iver nature center with
us.
    Anyway, lets get onto what happened. The course was so fun.
    In the maze, the first time we were in the maze
    Everyone was all together and then we all lost each other.
    But then we found each other and we found are way out.
    The woodland was relly nice. It was so lovely and pretty.
    And we relly liked drawing the flowers. It was atchly very
    Tricky. But we had a relly good time. Everybody loved
    Lunch time. Are food was relly nice. Oh, me and sam
    For got to ask what did all of you have for lunch?
    Alright, now I am going to tell you how much fun I had.
    You already know how much fun I had. But it was the
    Best school trip ever. In the meadow there was a lovely,
    Pretty bee. It was getting some of that stuff to make honey.

      Thank you for having all of beech class.

      From everybody.xxx

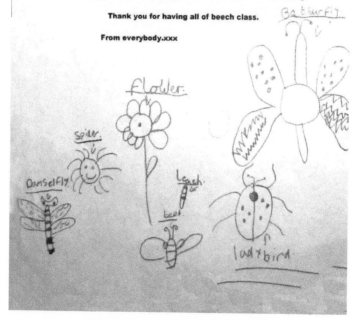

Thank-You Letter From 'Beech Class'

which could be used by those whose reading skills were limited.

The woodland at Iver was tiny but it was surprising what could be found in it, especially under the floor debris. The session began with the children standing under the trees, eyes closed, listening to woodland sounds which were different to those of the open meadow. They then looked for minibeasts around the trees, under leaves and in dead wood.

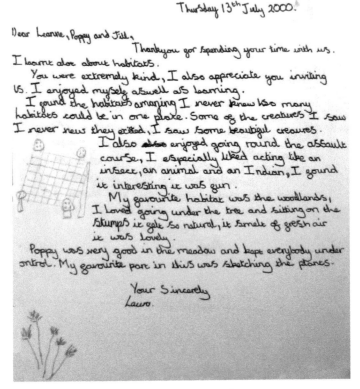

Thursday 13th July 2000.

Dear Leanne, Poppy and Jill,

Thankyou for spending your time with us. I learnt alot about habitats.

You were extremely kind, I also appreciate you inviting us. I enjoyed myself aswell as learning.

I found the habitats amazing I never knew so many habitats could be in one place. Some of the creatures I saw I never knew they existed, I saw some beautiful creatures.

I also enjoyed going round the assault course, I especially liked acting like an insect, an animal and an Indian, I found it interesting it was fun.

My favourite habitat was the woodlands, I loved going under the tree and sitting on the stumps it felt so natural, it smelt of fresh air it was lovely.

Poppy was very good in the meadow and kept everybody under control. My favourite part in this was sketching the plants.

Your Sincerely
Laura.

Thank-You Letter From Laura

Volunteer Kareth Paterson used a 'pet' snail for observational skills, asking questions such as, 'From its centre, in which direction does the spiral on the shell swirl - clockwise or anticlockwise?' 'Where are a snail's eyes?' 'Do snails have a nose to smell with?' 'Do they have teeth?' 'How do snails move if they have no feet?'

Every spring, three small snails were removed from the vegetable plot as youngsters and all lived in well-fed, snail heaven with Kareth for the season. Once each became used to being handled, it was usually most cooperative to pop its head out when a child stroked the shell. At the end of the school term, 'Bonzo', named by the first school, and his understudies, all now mature snails, were removed to the far end of the Centre, well away from the vegetable patch. No doubt they used their incredible homing instinct to return to the place of their birth.

After completing a tree bark rubbing, using paper and a crayon, the children then looked at leaves to compare colour, shape, texture etc. Finally, each child looked for a fallen leaf of their choice, examining its size, shape, colour and pattern carefully before placing it in a box containing an assortment of leaves which had been collected from all around the gardens. Before the children returned to school, the box of assorted leaves was emptied on to a worktable for each child to identify his or her leaf, with ninety-eight per cent being successful. If they wanted, they could keep their special leaf – most did.

One day, Kareth had a group of eight year olds around a tree and, before the bark-rubbing activity took place, asked, "What is the protective covering of a tree called?"

No response.

"It sounds like the noise a dog would make," she offered.

"Woof," came the reply!

As the years passed, volunteers Kareth Paterson, Hazel Hook and Shelagh Patmore became experts at running this part of the package.

*

'The Science of Christmas' was another activity which proved extraordinarily popular. This covered electricity, candles, crackers, Christmas cards and Christmas puddings.

As an introduction, the electricity session covered role-playing circuits, using tennis balls, followed by actually making a circuit using a battery and a mini-light bulb. Next, each constructed a Christmas lantern, made from an old Christmas card, which was then hung on a Correx (a type of plastic) Christmas tree which the group took back to school.

Volunteer Poppy Thomas was the expert at running the candle activity. This began with an introduction to wax and how a beehive works, using the real thing but without the bees! It was followed by investigating the properties of a flame, when a real candle was lit then covered with an upturned glass to extinguish the flame. Usually, at this point, the group was transfixed. To finish, the participants rolled their own beeswax candle which they took home.

Kareth was the queen of Christmas puddings, made using a recipe she created especially for 'The Science of Christmas' and, during her years, must have been responsible

18/12/00

Dear Poppy, Kareth and cora,

Thank you very much for an enjoyable day at your iver nature study centre I have been inspired by the intellagence gone into your centre. The activitys are fab! and I would enjoy another go at everyone of them soon.

I particuly liked the christmas pudding making as I am going to try and make my own at christmas.

The candle making was very artistic and full of fun along with your great action game which was fantastic.

I now find that lights are very important in a traddional christmas.

All in all I had a ~ WONDERFULL day so thank you very much.

Yours Greatfully
Rachel

Thank-You Letter From Rachel

for overseeing hundreds being prepared. The session began with a brief history of the festive pudding then the children, working in twos, weighed, measured, grated and whisked the ingredients before adding each to the main baking bowl. After each child and helper had stirred the mixture three times while making a wish, it was then poured into foil containers to be cooked off-site.

To finish, the children were given named pictures of every ingredient and a list of countries where each was grown or made. Sitting around the edges of a large map of the world, working together, they then put each ingredient on its country of origin. By the time every picture had been placed, they were often amazed to find the ingredients had come from several areas of every continent except the Arctic and Antarctic.

The day normally finished with a rendition of the carol, 'The Twelve Days of Christmas', with the children forming a circle and each holding an A4-size laminated card which volunteer Mary Pomeroy had illustrated with an image of each of the twelve gifts given, e.g. a partridge in a pear tree, five gold rings, pipers piping, lords a-leaping etc. When their character was sung, the children holding that picture rushed into the middle of the circle, held it up then returned to their place. The child holding the partridge in a pear tree had his/her work cut out because they were running in and out from verse one right through until verse twelve. The first time was usually chaotic but they always clamoured for another go which ran much more smoothly.

Throughout the years, we also held open days, monthly

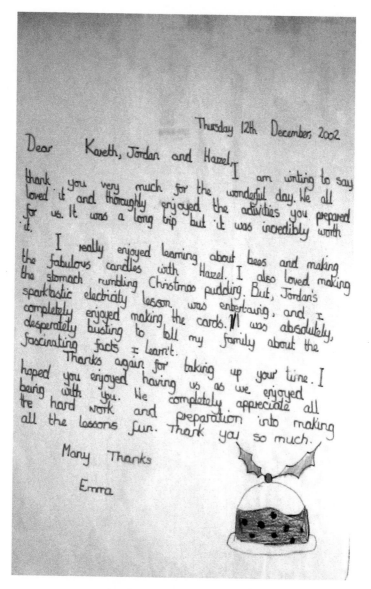

Thursday 12th December, 2002

Dear Kaveth, Jordan and Hazel,

I am writing to say thank you very much for the wonderful day. We all loved it and thoroughly enjoyed the activities you prepared for us. It was a long trip but it was incredibly worth it.

I really enjoyed learning about bees and making the fabulous candles with Hazel. I also loved making the stomach rumbling Christmas pudding. But, Jordan's sparktastic electricity lesson was entertaining, and I completely enjoyed making the cards. I was absolutely, desperately busting to tell my family about the fascinating facts I learnt.

Thanks again for taking up your time. I hoped you enjoyed having us as we enjoyed being with you. We completely appreciate all the hard work and preparation into making all the lessons fun. Thank you so much.

Many Thanks

Emma

Thank-You Letter From Emma

21

strolls around the Centre, art classes and craft sessions, all with a natural history theme. However, the activities which were enjoyed above and beyond everything else were the 'Experiences' and now, as well as writing about these, I feel it is time to introduce, in more detail, some of the people who, without doubt, made it possible for the Centre to offer the diversity of activities it became known for; the Iver Nature Study Centre Volunteer Team.

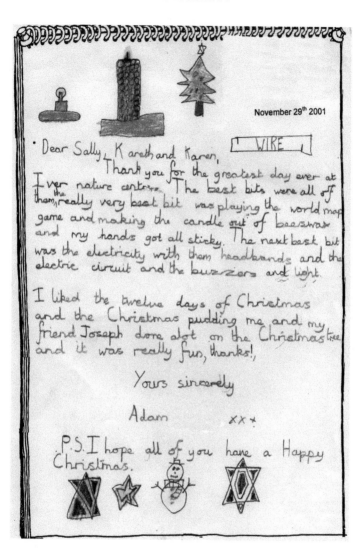

November 29th 2001

• Dear Sally, Kareth and Karen,

Thank you for the greatest day ever at I ver nature centre. The best bits were all of them, the really very best bit was playing the world map game and making the candle out of beeswax and my hands got all sticky. The next best bit was the electricity with them headbands and the electric circuit and the buzzers and light.

I liked the twelve days of Christmas and the Christmas pudding me and my friend Joseph done alot on the Christmas tree and it was really fun, thanks!,

Yours sincerely

Adam   xx +

P.S. I hope all of you have a Happy Christmas.

Thank-You Letter From Adam

TWO

VOLUNTEERS AND 'EXPERIENCES'
THE LADIES IN THE OFFICE

INTRODUCING SOME OF INSC'S MANY VOLUNTEERS ALONG
WITH DETAILS OF OUR 'EXPERIENCES'.
THE LADIES WHO HELPED ORGANISE BOTH THE OFFICE
AND ME.

Where do I begin to sing the praises of the most extraordinary group of people I have had the pleasure of knowing over the past three decades?

The sign at the bottom of the lane which led to the Centre seemed to draw a certain type of person. Many were from what is now commonly referred to as 'The Greatest Generation' – those born or living between 1939 and 1954; the war years and the end of rationing. As I got to know them, what came across was that they showed incredibly similar characteristics. Namely, they were all individuals, holding their own beliefs and doing their own thing, yet each had the self-determination to be responsible for their own life and deal with their problems.

In the early days, before risk assessments, health and safety, grievance procedures etc, people offering their help would drop in and we would have an initial chat, usually over a cup of tea. Once I found out what they were good at, they started immediately. One long-serving volunteer likened my technique to that of a praying mantis! Over the years, they never seemed to say 'no' when asked to do something. "We daren't", one devoted volunteer was heard to lament.

Not long after Keith's arrival, Kerstin Schrottke, who hailed from Germany, turned up at the Centre, out of the blue, wanting to volunteer. She was highly intelligent, hard-working and had a wonderful artistic skill which meant, for the first year, I had someone who could bring my ideas to fruition. She not only stayed with my family for nine months to improve her English but also became, and still is, a personal friend.

What was interesting to watch over the years was the gradual drawing together of the 'hard core' group of volunteers who were always there when the call, 'Your Centre Needs You!' went out. It was to their credit, so many people, with such diverse personalities and differing abilities, got on together. However, the common denominator which ran through the whole team was them being caring and compassionate people; the 'givers' in life.

Introducing some of INSC's many volunteers, along with details of our 'Experiences'

In 1994, the first 'Experience' was born. I wanted to create a rainforest in the small activity room where visitors could walk along a path surrounded by foliage, pass the scene of the forest being cut down then go over a bridge which would have water beneath it.

This was when Sue Taylor first appeared. She worked in a local day-care centre and her name had been given to me as someone who might be able to help with the painting of the rainforest being destroyed. She had an amazing artistic talent, completely self-taught. "People like me didn't go to art college," she once said. More often than not, when the official opening of an 'Experience' was underway, with dignitaries and guests touring the exhibition, Sue would still be adding last-minute touches and, invariably, covered in paint!

Another prodigiously talented volunteer was Geoff Thomas, who eventually became Iver's part-time gardener. He helped to construct the rainforest and even persuaded his talented mother to create a toucan and a parrot.

In 1994, 'The Rainforest Experience' was opened by Rocky, a blue and gold macaw, and we managed to have Baloo and King Louis costume-characters, of Disney's The Jungle Book film fame, visit the exhibition.

My initial small band of volunteers was skilful and enthusiastic. I used these assets when we put on this first public 'Experience' which would teach both our adult visitors and school children a little about the rainforests of South America.

To help create the feel of a rainforest, a local firm donated two bolts of fabric, each with jungle and flower patterns which we used as the backdrop to disguise the pine walls of the activity room. Once those were in place, a replica jungle was constructed, with features including a buttress tree root and a wooden bridge across a pretend river which contained water. Within the jungle was a variety of both hand-made and purchased models of birds, insects and animals. These included a toucan, an iguana, a green amazon parrot, a cayman, poison dart frogs, a millipede, a snake, papier-mâché fungi and a life-sized photograph of a jaguar's head, the latter being cleverly camouflaged by the thick vegetation. Children from two local schools in the Uxbridge area made dozens of colourful paper butterflies which were placed throughout. On one wall, the large mural, painted by Sue, depicting loggers destroying the forest, often came as quite a shock to our visitors. There was also a river scene, housed in a box which was viewed through the cabin window.

Three quarters of the vegetation was real. The Royal Botanical Gardens, Kew, generously gave us their discarded debris from the Palm House, together with some larger varieties of tropical plants which really brought the jungle to life and we also received gifts of tropical plants from several companies.

After visitors had toured the rainforest, with a tape of rainforest noises playing in the background, we offered a variety of activities, each suitable for the group visiting that day. For the younger visitors, these included an 'I Spy' worksheet, followed by a talk about what the rainforest gives us by way of fruit, vegetables and medicines. Everyone was told about the many layers which are found in these tropical rainforests, plus a few interesting facts about some of the animals and insects which live there. Thanks to the generosity of a local supermarket donating tropical fruit for each week of the run, our feely box, containing six types of rainforest fruit, was very popular, particularly with the children who, after working out what each fruit was, were offered a sample to eat.

Older children and other visitors, following their tour, discussed factors affecting rainforest destruction and occasionally took part in role playing, having been allocated the parts of government official, loggers, farmers, scientists, rainforest inhabitants etc, discussing the pros and cons for keeping/destroying the rainforests.

Whenever possible, we also had live animals visit! These included a blue and gold macaw, a brightly coloured Red-lored amazon parrot, royal pythons, a baby boa constrictor, tree frogs, a tortoise and a few bird-eating spiders, all of which, needless to say, caused great excitement.

Our visitors included the Society of Disabled Artists, a local stroke club, various children's WATCH groups, Brownie packs, youth clubs, school children, special needs groups, our regular day care centre groups and about two hundred visiting members of the public. In all, we welcomed just under fifteen hundred people to this first of what would, over the years, be three 'Rainforest Experiences'. I am sure you can imagine the planning it took for this first 'Experience' but the effort was worth it and I had a superb team of volunteers, without whose support and enthusiasm, none of the above would have been possible.

Graham Myers, a former maths teacher who wanted to

work in the environmental field, volunteered at the Centre for a year to gain experience. He was brilliant at teaching children about rainforests.

The education pack for this 'Rainforest Experience' included using a very large painting showing the different layers of the forest, from ground-level undergrowth, upwards through each storey, to the highest tree tops emerging into the open sky. Although this worked well, as time went by, we used the children to depict the forest layers which was much more fun and, I have to say, they retained far more than when they just watched and listened.

Two children would be chosen to lie on the ground, depicting the forest floor, then two or three small children would sit upright behind them, as the shrub, or understorey layer. Next, as the canopy, were slightly taller children, kneeling and with arms outstretched in front of them, casting shadows over the understorey and forest floor. Finally, the two tallest standing, arms outstretched upward into the air, were the emergent layer.

The class, using worksheet support, would then explore the actual jungle, looking at the different shaped leaves and for the animals and birds hiding in the foliage. Food chains were introduced, using a paste-and-stick activity. The lifestyle of the rainforest people was compared to their own, after which causes and reasons were discussed as to why rainforests were under threat. Hands-on activities included mask-making, egg shell mosaics and creating a rainforest collage, all of which the children took back to school.

The first 'Rainforest Experience' proved so popular, almost three years later, in 1997, we went on to create a larger version, this time in the newly extended visitors' cabin. This one was opened by Jackie Zammit of 'The Rainforest Roadshow' and attracted over two thousand visitors during its eleven-week run. But I am getting ahead of myself.

*

During the summer of 1994, Peter Hinson and his wife, Gwen, became regular volunteers. Gwen had visited the Centre to recycle a bag of pond weed and, in the course of conversation, let it be known that Peter was very artistic. She had hardly returned home before I telephoned, asking for help! Thus began a unique partnership. Not only was Peter hands-on with all the 'Experiences' but, whenever I needed advice, a poster designed for an event, some graphics for worksheets, or the Centre's annual Christmas card, it was he who provided the answers. He even volunteered to play Father Christmas when we created a Christmas grotto and, for his pains, caught an eyeful of fake snow during the photo call! When an 'Experience' was in full swing, Gwen would always be on hand to clear up the mess we all made.

*

In 1995, we followed the first 'Rainforest Experience' with 'The Sea Experience', this time transforming the activity room into an underwater scene, complete with hundreds of paper cut-out fish hanging from the ceiling and, courtesy of Sue, a kelp forest, together with an octopus and a shark, created by Peter, which were seen through a small window.

Photo: Children looking up at the kelp forest.
©Sally Munn

I asked Keith if he would make me a life-size jigsaw of a blue whale. He actually hesitated then said 'no' but, two weeks later, came back with a diagram and details of how he was going to create such an enormous mammal which averages thirty-five metres (115 feet) in length. He cut out twenty-three pieces of hardboard with a jigsaw. Peter, using his artistic skills, painted the detail on the head and 'The Tuesday Volunteers' (more of whom later) painted the main body. Visiting school children took great delight in carrying each piece of the whale then laying them out, in the correct position, in the Centre's car park. The entire class would then join hands along the length of the completed jigsaw which gave them some idea of the vast scale of the largest mammal on Earth.

Whale jigsaw in the Study Centre's car park.
©National Grid plc and with kind permission of The Groundwork South
Trust (2020).

Tracy Edwards MBE, who skippered the first all-female yacht crew in the Whitbread Round the World Race, kindly opened this 'Experience'.

Roll forward eleven years to June, 2006 when fifty-four children, along with teachers and seventeen parents, arrived on a school trip to learn about the 'Sea and Seashore'. It seemed the parents were very keen to be part of this trip.

I was approached at the start of the day by a seven-year-old girl who told me she knew all about both the Centre and me. I asked if she had visited before. 'No,' replied the child. "My mummy came here when she was a little girl and she told me all about Iver Nature Study Centre."

It was at that point I thought, perhaps I had been there too long!

*

After 'The Sea Experience', we went on to create 'The Culture and Customs of Native American Plains and Woodlands Indians' project which became known as 'The Native American Indian Experience' (1996), the second 'Rainforest Experience' (1997), 'The African Experience' (1998), the permanent, outdoor 'Rainforest Experience' (1999), '2001: A Space Experience' then our final major project, 'Dig for Victory' (2005) which celebrated the Home Front for the sixtieth anniversary of the ending of WWII. The following are outlines and highlights from each.

*

Nothing seemed to faze the volunteers. For 'The Native American Indian Experience', Keith built a wigwam and a totem pole in the woodland area. In the meadow, a large tepee was erected, on one side of which Peter painted a buffalo.

I telephoned Sue. "Sue, I need a life-sized buffalo."

"Yes, of course. Male or female?"

I then contacted the Natural History Museum, London, requesting anatomical details for constructing an adult buffalo, much to the astonishment of the gentleman from that department. Fortunately, he responded to my unusual request and, from the details he sent, Sue was able to construct our buffalo to the correct size, shape and appearance.

From a wooden skeleton, constructed by Keith, followed by wire, hosepipe, rugs, bits of carpet and the contents of many tubes of 'Polyfilla'™, used by Sue, a staggeringly life-

33

The buffalo in our meadow
©Sally Munn

like, full-sized buffalo materialised which stood majestically in the meadow for many years. It was used to explain how important the animal was for the Plains Indians' lifestyle.

On to 1997 and now with a new extension giving us two extra activity rooms, I decided, after the success of the first, to put on a second 'Rainforest Experience'. Again, my team came up with the goods, turning the larger room into a tropical forest, along the same lines as the first but more extensive.

There was enough space to build a three-dimensional buttress tree, complete with twisting green stems, around and through which a variety of tropical plants were growing. This was situated at the beginning of the path which then wound its way through thick and overhanging foliage. When you looked around, a few animals would be staring back at you! There was a lifelike, painted waterfall, created by Peter, above which a python hung from a branch of thick foliage over the 'pond' which represented a river.

Further along the path, we had a live iguana in a camouflaged glass tank, provided by volunteers Vic and Jan who kept exotic pets. Towards the end of the tour, visitors came to a village hut, surrounded by bamboo and greenery. Here, Jackie Zammit from 'The Rainforest Roadshow', who had opened this current 'Experience', held court, answering any questions the children and visitors had about rainforests.

The activities we provided for visiting school and other groups remained more or less the same as for the previous 'Rainforest Experience', having proven to be popular with everyone.

Peter's proposed design for the painting of the waterfall
©Peter Hinson

As before, we were busy with visitors, school outings, special needs groups and occasional visitors who were curious, most having read about it in the local newspapers.

Next came 'The African Experience' which opened in 1998 and was very popular. The complete frontage to the main cabin was hidden behind a plywood screen, painted by volunteer Barry Reid, to resemble the outside stonework of a pyramid, in front of which was a section of a round 'stone' (polystyrene) pillar on which was carved the head of an Egyptian pharaoh. There were also huge 'stone' pillars at the entrance, on which volunteer Muriel Caley had created wonderful hieroglyphics. To gain entry to the main room, visitors walked along the, now enclosed, verandah which had been transformed into a dim, 'stone' tunnel, resembling the entrance to the tomb of a pharaoh, then turned right, into the main activity room.

Peter had dressed the initial scene as a burial chamber. On the right-hand side, protected by a wire screen, lying on a bed of sand, was a jumbled display of grave relics. These included pieces of gold, amulets, jewellery pouring from an open gold box, eating utensils, oil lamps and, nearby, four Canopic jars which would have contained the body's internal organs and entrails. It was amazing to realise everything in this initial scene of riches had been created from papier-mâché, wood, recycled bits and bobs, glass beads, paper and the ingenuity of several volunteers.

Against the opposite wall was a sarcophagus and, propped upright beside it, an open coffin containing a wrapped mummy. The coffin had been constructed in volunteer, Ian Pearce's garage at home, much to the consternation of the

Relics in the burial chamber
©Kareth Paterson

local postman who noticed it one morning as he approached their front door!

Emerging from the tomb into the main activity room, attached to the walls, was a painted mural so large, it covered the length and height of one long and one short wall. Sue, again using her creative talents, had transformed the first half into the Sahara desert, in front of which Peter had created a painted, cut-out hardboard camel, ridden by a man dressed in Arab robes. Further along, it depicted the Serengeti plains, a small village, sparsely-leafed bushes, trees and lifelike animals, including a herd of wildebeest. On the shorter wall, Peter had painted a hardboard cut-out of an elephant with her calf emerging from a stand of trees. In front of this was a small platform, camouflaged by tufts of scrub and grasses,

Elephant with calf and lioness with cub
© Kareth Paterson

on which was a lioness with a cub in her mouth; toy ones but almost life-sized.

In the tropical rainforest scene was a variety of papier-mâché, plastic and carved wooden African birds, insects, animals and reptiles, most of which were partially hidden from view by tree branches and lush foliage.

For the opening day's entertainment, we had a five-man African drumming group and Sheila Grey, a local policewoman, gave an energetic exhibition of belly dancing which was a big hit with everyone. As a dancer, her professional name was Jaiyed Naviz, meaning 'good wine'.

When 'The African Experience' came to an end, we put the pyramid to good use when Barry transformed it into a giant scoreboard and we launched our own coverage of

'World Cup 98', using this to promote literacy, numeracy, geography and healthy eating.

*

In 1999, we constructed a permanent rainforest in a polytunnel in the Study Centre's garden, where we could continuously offer this popular and important subject.

This ambitious project not only had all the elements of the two indoor rainforest exhibitions but, with so much space to fill, the volunteers again designed, experimented, handmade and put together a life-like South American rainforest, complete with a wooden bridge over running water which was home to live fish. Camouflaged in the

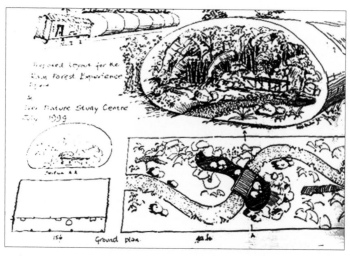

Peter's proposed design for the outdoor polytunnel rainforest
©Peter Hinson

greenery were models of a life-sized anaconda snake, birds, animals, amphibians and insects. A CD of rainforest sounds played in the background, making it even more authentic. On hot days, volunteer Henry Avery, or one of the other volunteers, drenched the inside of the tunnel with the hose to create jungle humidity. The set-up was so realistic, our visitors felt they had been transported to a far-off land.

When Kareth was teaching children about the goods and foods which come from the rainforests, as well as discussing and tasting fruits, she talked about chocolate which brought them all to attention! After telling them there were bars of chocolate ranging from seventy-five per cent chocolate content, down to some with only twenty per cent, she asked which they would prefer. Of course, it was hands up for the seventy-five percent. She then asked which was their favourite

Inside the polytunnel rainforest
©Sally Munn

chocolate bar. To demonstrate the chocolate content of their, almost unanimous, favourite, using its purple wrapper, she folded it over and over until just twenty per cent remained on view. This showed the children what they much prefer are the milk and sugar but only a little chocolate which amazed each and every one of them.

Throughout every 'Experience', the regular volunteers gave their time, expertise and enthusiasm to make each a success. Before beginning a major project, I only ever held one meeting, which never lasted for more than an hour. I would tell the volunteers what I envisaged and, within that hour, Peter would already be designing the layout, Kareth and Hazel sorting the education package, Geoff calculating what materials were needed to build everything, Poppy, Sue

Thank-you letter from Luke

and Ian discussing how they would do the 'bits in the middle' and volunteers Lily Harris, Lynne Avery, Elizabeth Whiting and Chris Hare deciding what catering was required for the launch. My responsibilities included getting sponsorship, seeing to publicity and providing the materials the volunteers requested to create the project.

There was always a great atmosphere when we were creating an 'Experience', with everyone pulling together and helping each other. The ingenuity used to overcome problems was astounding and rarely did anyone put in a claim for materials they had bought themselves. Poppy would get very angry when asked for receipts. "I didn't get one!" was her normal, forceful reply.

*

'2001: A Space Experience' was really special in what was achieved. Geoff's face was a picture when I asked him if he would not only build a scale model of a space shuttle but create the Iver National Space Centre which had the same acronym as Iver Nature Study Centre i.e. INSC. Peter Hill, from National Grid, generously provided us with space in one of their workshops where volunteers, Ron Munn and Barry helped Geoff to construct the model. It was also here where Barry sculpted both the body and nose cone of the orbiter from polystyrene.

The Space Centre was created inside the marquee.

Volunteer Ian Pearce's wife, Mary, admitted she was not artistic but willingly picked up a brush to paint the panels which made up the walls dividing the various activity areas.

An amusing story emerged after our initial Support Group meeting at the start of the year to organise '2001: A Space Experience'. One of the team, who shall remain nameless to save any embarrassment, knocked on my office door.

"I'm concerned about launching our shuttle. Heathrow

Space shuttle *Iverana* in the car park
©Sally Munn

is only a few miles away and my son says we would never be given permission."

Trying to contain my laughter, I explained ours was a mock-up space shuttle which, although it would look the genuine thing, would not be capable of flying, let alone taking off!

When it was erected in the main car park, where it took pride of place in front of the visitors' cabin, the scaled-down model did look incredibly realistic so perhaps said volunteer had the foresight to recognise just how authentic our 'Experiences' were.

While the model shuttle's construction was underway, we realised, like the real thing, it would need a name, but what? I asked for suggestions and one volunteer came up with Iveranae, going on to explain 'ranae' was Latin for frog which appropriately, was Iver's logo. Perfect, but we adapted it to *Iverana* to make it unique.

While the heavy construction work went on, twins, Laura and Katie Ferrin, after spending time with us on work experience, became part of the team helping our special needs groups. For 'Space', as a group, with Cora [Cloughley] Hossain, that year's National Grid graduate's, help, they designed and produced 'Discovering the Final Frontier', a huge handmade mural which took up most of a wall in the visitors' cabin. The timeline of space exploration through the years was easy to follow by means of a path of gold stars, cut-out space ships, satellites, moons and planets, interspersed with typed pages of interesting facts.

The education team originally comprised of seven, until volunteer Joyce Jones had to bow out prior to the opening.

'Discovering the Final Frontier' mural
©Sally Munn

Each of us had an astronaut's uniform which was worn whenever a group visited to take part in 'Space' activities. Mine, as Commander Sally, was green; the astronauts and payload specialists were white, and we all wore white trainers. On each uniform, Poppy made, then attached, machine-embroidered badges, plus our unique Mission logo which Peter designed. Kareth fund-raised enough to provide each of us with a white baseball cap, on the front of which was embroidered '2001: A Space Experience'. We also had white space helmets which, in reality, were motorbike safety helmets.

When we were up and running, visitors were shown to a seating area in the marquee where they watched the launch of *Iverana*. My younger son, Jamie, a film editor, had created the launch film which included scenes of the seven Iver

The Iver National Space Centre astronauts with their mission logo
©Kareth Paterson

National Space Centre astronauts during lift-off. It was so authentic, many children and several adults were convinced they were watching the real thing.

After watching *Iverana*'s lift off, everyone left the 'cinema' to enter then walk through outer space; a long, dim passage which represented the solar system. This was faintly illuminated by stars twinkling across the heavens and planets, all made by Sue and Ian, and suspended from the black ceiling. At the far end of the tunnel was the large, dramatic backdrop of our sun, painted by Barry. Visitors then turned right to enter the brightly lit Space Station, housed in the other half of the marquee. Here, they learned about the planets, gravity,

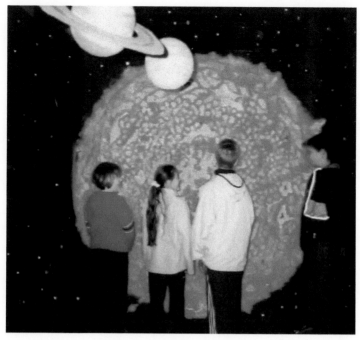

Children looking at the sun
©Sally Munn

explored the tiny living and sleeping areas for the astronauts, saw food packs and were always astonished by the cramped conditions endured by those on a space mission.

Kareth, who was a whizz on the computer, designed a space passport cum mission log, a copy of which was given to each child who took part in the various group activities we ran over the months of the 'Experience'. At the start of their day, before entering the Space Centre marquee, we measured then noted each child's height in their log. At the end of their visit, before returning their mission log, now officially

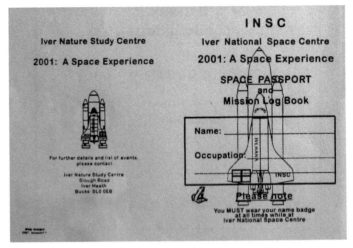

The Space Centre's mission log (outside)
©Kareth Paterson

stamped with each activity they had undertaken, their height was again measured and noted, but this time at the exit door.

Over the course of their day with our team of astronauts – Poppy, Hazel, Kareth, Cora and my then, part-time secretary/occasional volunteer, Jill Myers – each group learned about sleeping, eating, washing and of course, the answer to the most frequent question of all: how do astronauts go to the loo while weightless?

With Cora's enthusiastic approach to teaching, the children had fun experimenting with gravity and, on a few occasions, making rocket fuel to launch plastic bottle spaceships across the meadow. There were some small but significant facts they found very interesting. Firstly, the 'Velcro' strips which fastened their trainers, anoraks, school satchels etc. are also used in outer space to anchor items which would otherwise float around in the gravity-free atmosphere. Secondly, learning the long, back seam of every space suit was secured by a strip of 'Velcro', making getting in and out, while wearing thick, warm, under clothing and gloves, much easier and thirdly, having a strip of 'Velcro' low down in their visor, officially helped clear their ears during pressure changes and, unofficially, also made a great nose-scratcher.

At the end of their day in 'space', when each child had their height measured against the tape measure at the exit from the Space Centre marquee, they were thrilled to learn they had gained at least 2.5 cms /1 in which was then noted in their mission log!

Before leaving the Centre, they were advised, by the time

Please fill in this section	**Missions undertaken while at INSC**
Name:	1.
Boy or Girl:	
Age (if under 18):	2.
Date of Birth (if under 18):	3.
Colour of Eyes:	
Colour of Hair:	4.
Height: _____ Cm	

FOR OFFICIAL USE ONLY	**Signatures of Space Commander, Astronauts and/or Payload Specialists at INSC**
Height after 2001: A Space Experience	
_____ Cm	1. _____ 2. _____
Please note	3. _____ 4. _____
Any increase in your height is temporary. Earth's gravity will return you to your usual height.	

The Space Centre's mission log (inside)

©Kareth Paterson

they reached home, because of the force of gravity on planet Earth, they would have returned to their normal height – much to their disappointment.

During the run, we had a visit from American astronaut Dr Don Lind who, while based at Mission Control in Houston, Texas, had been a payload specialist for the Apollo 11 moon landing in 1969.

After watching the film of our space shuttle *Iverana*'s take-off, Dr Lind gave a very interesting talk to a packed audience, telling us how in 1985, as Mission Specialist, he finally achieved his life's ambition to fly in outer space. Using our film screen, he showed us a wonderful selection of slides he had taken while completing 110 orbits of Earth over his seven days, eight minutes and forty-six seconds as a crew member onboard the orbiter *Challenger*. After touring the Iver National Space Centre, he remarked on how impressed he was at what we had created.

*

Two days after Iver's eleventh anniversary which, that year, fell on Friday, 21 September, the final day of '2001: A Space Experience' on the Sunday coincided with our annual Open Day.

After the last visitor left and everything had been cleaned and put away, we 'Iverites' enjoyed a 'family supper' in the activities area of the marquee which had been our Space Centre for so many months. Following our meal, while the tables were cleared and dishes removed to the kitchen, Cora, Hazel and Kareth changed into their space suits and baseball caps, to become usherettes with torches for showing everyone to a seat in the 'cinema' area which visitors entered first. Once seated and settled, for the final time, there was a showing of the *Iverana* launch; the film made by my son, Jamie. While everyone was watching it, I slipped out, dashed to my office, returning minutes later as the credits rolled, dressed all in black, as an ice cream lady, complete with torch in one hand and tray of ices suspended around my neck! What made my volunteers laugh even more was watching me trying to hand out ice creams to everyone whilst my white, lacy cap continually slipped over my eyes! While I, half-blind, doled out ice creams, Peter surprised everyone by materialising from behind the wooden partition at the entrance to the marquee with a portable organ, à la 'the organist entertains'! After the laughter died down, we had a jolly good sing-song, followed by a celebratory glass of champagne. Although we were sad to see the last of 'Space', the evening turned into one of the most hilarious at INSC but also closed the chapter of what had undoubtedly, been our most ambitious 'Experience' to date.

The following year, a young lad visiting the Centre with his school, after dropping off his lunch bag in the big bin, came up to me.

"You're Commander Sally!" he exclaimed in astonishment.

"Yes, you're quite right. I was Commander Sally last year. Did you enjoy your 'Space' adventure?"

"Yes, it was great," he replied.

"Tell me something you learned during your visit."

"I learned how to wash my hands properly," he replied, in all seriousness.

I no longer recall my response to his answer but do hope it is something he will continue to do for the rest of his life.

Our '2001: A Space Experience' project ran for five months, with over four thousand people either visiting or taking part in activities.

*

Having said that would be the last extravaganza I would ask the team to undertake –we were all older and wiser– in 2005, I could not let the sixtieth anniversary of the ending of WWII go by without acknowledging the debt we owe that generation.

'Dig for Victory' was created to pay tribute to those who endured the Home Front during these perilous times. In the marquee, Geoff, Barry and Peter pulled out all the stops, with

1940's kitchen
©Sally Munn

Geoff building a 1940's kitchen and sitting room, complete with a Morrison shelter.

Barry produced the dramatic Blitz scene with a painted backdrop of bombed buildings, in front of which were piled the broken remains of what had once been family homes. Peter also made an exhibit showing what was happening during the actual war between 1939 and 1945 and I produced a photographic display of the Home Front.

Behind the marquee, an Anderson shelter was constructed next to the chicken run (with lifelike model chickens) and a newly created vegetable patch dug out and planted by Jill and Tony Myers. Later in the season, we harvested some of the produce which had grown so well over the summer.

Kareth produced our unique version of the National Registration Identity Card for the education package which included a line for the child's name along with a box to be

1940's sitting room with Morrison shelter
©Sally Munn

completed for each activity undertaken. These included the introduction to 'Dig for Victory', rationing, make do and mend, creating collages depicting the Home Front and making carrot buns to a WWII recipe, adapted from the recipe in her grandmother's war time cookery book. Over the months of this 'Experience', almost a thousand carrot buns were made and eaten! Kareth recently told me she still makes them, although now, only by the dozen.

We held a very special open day for anyone local who had experienced the Home Front. During this, we sang wartime

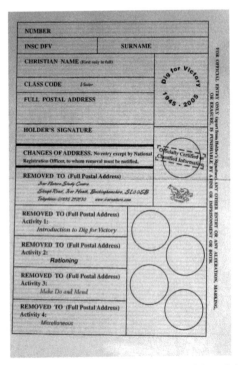

'Dig for Victory' WWII Identity Card (inside)

©Kareth Paterson

songs, had lunch then heard about what these people had endured and yet were still able to keep their sense of humour. Our guest of honour was former Spitfire pilot and television presenter, Raymond Baxter OBE, who then spent the entire afternoon talking with the guests. A delightful gentleman. I treasure the thank-you letter he sent following his visit, in which he complemented us for not only putting on 'Dig for Victory' but also for bringing those years to the attention of today's young people.

During the run of 'Dig for Victory', I thought it would be a great opportunity to have a fund-raising dinner and dance. In keeping with the wartime theme, I decided to call it 'In the Mood' and guests would be encouraged to come dressed in 1940's style. The response was marvellous. Many came in service uniforms, representing the armed forces of army, navy and air force personnel. Other outfits included a Bevin boy miner, several WLA (Women's Land Army) girls, nurses, an air raid warden, an American soldier, a school boy, 1940's housewives and a smattering of German army personnel and Luftwaffe crew.

The table decorations for the evening were handmade by the talented Mary Pomeroy and Peter designed the 'In the Mood' menu. Car parking, table clearing, keeping the urn topped up and helping with washing-up were carried out by the Middlesex & North West London Army Cadet Force, Uxbridge, who did a sterling job. Many from my volunteer team were on hand as runners throughout the evening.

The catering team included volunteers Kareth Paterson, Hazel Hook, Jackie Naughton, Glynis Hardy, Cherry Hammond, Gerry Alexander, Clare Bill, Nigel Phillips, Jenny

Pearson, Christine Morgan, Trish Antoun and Liz Pinfold, the latter two doing amazing things with a large bottle of modern-day 'Fairy Liquid' and dozens of tea towels, in the kitchen after each course.

To ensure a smooth running order and be confident we could fit everything in, all the volunteers had a copy of the timetable which used the twenty-four hour format.

1930 hours: While Jackie N signed everyone in on arrival, several volunteers sold raffle tickets and mixed with the guests.

The bar – manned by my son, Stewart, together with two of his work colleagues, Melanie Blackwell and Tammy Kidd – were kept busy serving drinks while, in the background, Perry Parson's Big Band played 1940s music.

2000 hours: As Master of Ceremonies, I gave my welcome speech, followed by the outline of how the evening would work. I also announced, should there be an air raid warning, everyone was to walk – (not run!) to the air-raid shelter (the main cabin) and remain there until the 'all clear' was sounded.

2015 hours: The raucous air-raid siren took everyone by surprise when it went off close by. No sooner had it stopped than an incredibly realistic drone of dozens of aircraft, followed by the deep booms and blasts of exploding bombs surrounded the Centre. With a little chivvying from Nicholas Smith, my Co-Master of Ceremonies, after asking everyone to push their chair under their table for safety reasons, he and the Army Cadets, who had previously helped with car parking duties, then led everyone, at walking pace, to the air-raid shelter. On arrival in the main activity room, the catering team, comprising of Jackie, Hazel and a couple of volunteers handed out the first course: a tea plate of mixed salad which included half a small egg and sprinkling of Cheddar cheese (both rationed items). After the first couple of dozen had collected their starter, the 'all clear' was sounded, allowing the guests to continue through the cabin, exit by the far door then return to the marquee.

2030 hours. Nicholas requested an orderly queue to form then led the first crocodile from the marquee back to the air-raid shelter where the smaller activity room had been transformed into a 1940's field kitchen, complete with catering-sized gas cookers. Here, Kareth and Hazel, with help from volunteers when they needed extra hands, had cooked the main course of the evening and heated the dinner plates. Dressed as canteen girls, they served each

Jackie N and Hazel plating 105 starters.
©Kareth Paterson

of our hundred plus guests with their main course of the wartime dish of 'Lord Woolton Pie'. The original recipe consisted of a variety of seasonal root vegetables, cauliflower plus their leaves, spring onions (ordinary onions were only a memory) and parsley plus stalks, none of which were on ration, vegetable extract, oatmeal to thicken and all to be cooked in a thin vegetable gravy then topped with thin pastry. The recipe for wartime pastry sounded so unpalatable, we offered potatoes instead, mashed with a little milk and butter, both the latter being on ration and, as a concession to the celebration, we thickened the runny sauce with a well-known modern gravy powder. As a treat, each guest was allowed two sausages (on ration) and also given extra gravy, if requested.

While our guests enjoyed a leisurely main course, with quiet background music provided by the band, back in the visitors' cabin large activity room, the catering team were busy organising the puddings. These consisted of stewed apples and stewed rhubarb, most of the latter from the garden of local Uxbridge resident and Iver supporter, Valerie Cook. To accompany these, each table was given a jug of custard and a tin of evaporated milk, along with an old-fashioned tin opener. Nigel and Kareth between them also provided carrot buns, made using Kareth's WWII recipe. While guests enjoyed their pudding in the marquee, back in the main activity room, volunteers cleared up while some cadets laid out everything for those who wanted tea or coffee after dinner. Several older guests, during the evening, remarked on how realistic everything was.

2145 hours: Announcements were made via recordings

from Downing Street and the Cabinet Office. Peace in Europe had been declared and the following two days would be a holiday. The round of applause and cheering from the guests raised the roof!

Prizes were then awarded to winners of the special numbered menu, a 'doctored' ID card and for the best-dressed person of the evening. This was followed by the raffle being drawn.

Perry Parson's Big Band now played music from the 1940's to the 1970's which had everyone up and dancing.

Midnight: The British national anthem, 'God Save the King' was sung and thus, the celebrations came to an end.

*

After the 'Dig for Victory' evening, Tony Cozens, who won first prize in the raffle, wrote a letter of thanks which I think sums up that night:

> Thank you, and all of your team …in one word, 'fantastic' …Both my wife and I have not enjoyed ourselves so much for ages …The meal was simply delicious …have never tasted such delicious sausages …I could not resist 'seconds' …The group we were seated with were so friendly … particularly Nigel and his wife …they all made us feel so welcome …
>
> …good to be able to dance properly to a great band … seeing such a young band restored my faith in the present generation …Perry Parsons deserves a lot of credit for keeping music 'live'.

I felt really proud to have my RAF uniform on again …I purchased my raffle tickets from a young lady wearing a Luftwaffe feldwebel's [sergeant's] uniform! …I won the raffle but felt your colleagues deserved to win more than we did!

Sally, thanks for a wonderful evening. It will live long in the memory …we felt sorry for you because you seemed to be dashing here, there and everywhere, making sure everything went smoothly …we hope you still had time to enjoy yourself …

Our thanks also to your staff …for helping to make the evening so memorable …[1]

I hope you have enjoyed the hour-by-hour detail of the above event. I thought it was a marvellous way to show how an extraordinary mixture of people gave of themselves, pulling together to make the dinner and dance such a success. All credit to them for having worked together and supported each other to make the evening, to quote Tony, 'memorable'.

*

Still full of ideas, once the 'Dig for Victory' dinner was over, I asked Geoff if, in a suitable area of the garden, he would design and construct 'The Olive Grove', complete with olive trees and an authentic pizza oven where we could cook our own pizzas. The result was a wonderful, hand-built, brick kiln and Geoff's friend, Bruno Carini, who owned an Italian

---

1   Letter extract with the kind permission of Tony Cozens' widow.
     ©Tony Cozens

restaurant, generously invented a recipe for the Iver pizza.

Children from the 'Growing with Gardening' Saturday morning scheme created a pretty mosaic table and also used their new skills to plant out the containers for the patio.

'The Olive Grove' project was kindly opened by Lady Lucinda Lambton.

*

It was not only the 'Experiences' when the volunteers came into their own. The running of the Centre required help for everything which went on there. By this time, we were not only catering to schools, special needs adults and children's units but also children's holiday play schemes, known as 'I'm Bored'. We had visits from holiday play clubs, Pyramid

'The Olive Grove'
©Geoff Thomas

Clubs, Girl Guides, Brownies, Boy Scouts, Cubs, Beavers, Girls' Brigade, Air and Sea Cadets, WIs, those on community service and several adult interest groups.

Every year, we took in work experience students, not only from schools and colleges but also those who were undertaking The Duke of Edinburgh's Award scheme. We wanted to give them all as much 'hands-on' experience as possible and, as volunteers, they proved to be exceedingly patient and supportive.

Geoff Thomas was of the old school and could put his hand to anything: gardening, carpentry, design work, sorting in-house problems and so on. His quiet, patient nature was marvellous with students on work experience, encouraging them all the time to achieve the task he had set, either with carpentry or in the garden.

What was gratifying was receiving frequent, wonderful thank-you cards and letters from many of the students saying, not only how much they had learned but also how much they had enjoyed themselves and how kind and supportive the regular INSC volunteers had been.

Because the original was too faint to reproduce successfully, the following is the transcription of the handwritten letter from David H in 1998.

Dear Sally,

I would like to thank you for allowing me to undertake my Work Experience with your organisation.

It has helped me gain a clearer idea of what it is like to be at work, and I learned a great deal about the job of a 'Nature Studier.'

The things I particularly enjoyed about the work experience were helping with the groups and talking with people and the fact that my preparation affected the enjoyment of the guest. Plus, of course, observing the moorhen family evolve!

Could you please thank everyone else who helped me whilst on Work Experience and gave their time to make my time with you so useful?

Finally, my Head of Careers, Mrs M ... has asked me to pass on her thanks and appreciation for your help.

Yours sincerely,
David H

The following is the accurate transcription of a most amusing but insightful thank-you letter from Martin, a young lad on work experience– and I did share the 'chocolats'.

To You

I just wanted to Say thanks for the two weeks work experience. Its been really good. 2 weeks ago I walked through Those big wooden gates not knowing what to expect or what i needed to do or what mysterious Creatures i would find in the wildlife. i later found one Called Sally Joking who at first was big and Scary but i tickled her funny bone and found the little kitten inside who i found out later on was more like a tiger, wild and always running about it was like She was doing the run from the benny hill Show. i was tempted to do the music but thought na but it was funny. As i settled in i met loads of new people who worked there. there was nigel who i would like to award the always finding Something i could do award too and also some lessons in life about how its fun to drive over humps in the road even when we've got 50 chairs in the back that was cool and also to Say thanks for all the help. then there was Jackie and while Sally was the wise granny goose Jackie was like a mum goose guiding me on what to do and to watch myself and get something to drink and it was like having your mum at work but a really cool mum. so Thanks and i will visit for your Birthday as your cake was nice mmm….. then there is Stewart who wasn't in for the first week but was a cool guy and looks a bit like a skinny Chris Moyles, I thought So thanks for all the help and all the weeding!

Then there are all the Volunteers who are cool. There's Henry who reminds me of the guys from dads army but he was funny and we made good bonfire, theres Jeff who i had a good time doing the pizza with. Thank you Bruno and also I have remembered Jeff that baby rabits are called Kittens thank you for the knowledge. theres Karith who was always laughing and smiling the same with hazel and My Mum would like to thank Lilly for teaching me how to work a kitchen which was new for me. But i'm gonna stop now Coz by the time you finnish it the phone will probably be ringing. Also quick mention for Dave who taught me alot and we also got alot of the Stuff from B 'n'Q moved and basicly thanks to everyone for everything and as i said i walked in a boy and have now left a man. so thanxs to everyone and Good Luck with everything you do with the Centre and in your lifes and you never know i mite see you in the Summer holidays

So thanks for everything
Martin
P.S. Sally don't take all the Chocolats

Sisters Katie and Laura Ferrin, then aged sixteen, came on work experience and learnt so much, they became part-time employees at the Centre, designing activities and running many of the adult special needs groups. They were lovely, gentle, hard-working girls who could be relied upon to do things right.

Introducing even more marvellous volunteers and helpers

Not long after I started, Bill Harris turned up for an outdoor tea dance which I had organised. We were standing together watching wheelchair users dancing and he asked me for more details about the Centre. During our chat, I mentioned about needing more people to keep the garden under control. Even though it was a wildlife area, health and safety meant we had to make sure it was safe for all users. He immediately volunteered to look after the vegetable patch, together with its 'inherited' special needs gardening volunteer group, known as 'The Tuesday Volunteers' because they came every Tuesday. The regulars included Simon Jeffries, Mike Linford, Raymond Kelliher, Ray Tuckwell, Mark Gardner and Pauline Guinn.

In the early days, I usually found Simon just standing around doing nothing. Speaking to him in the hope of finding out why he was not working, he told me he hated gardening.

"Why didn't you say when they put you in the gardening group?" I asked, somewhat surprised. "What would you like to do?"

"Wash the vehicles," he replied.

Simon eventually became the car and mini bus wash king, keeping them sparkling both inside and out.

Mike not only helped in the garden but also kept the tool shed tidy.

Pauline, as well as her gardening duties, became the mail shot queen.

Another 'Tuesday Volunteer' was Jeremy Cumming who was partially sighted. He was looked after by Tony Myers, an excellent car mechanic and also the husband of Jill who, at that time, was in charge of the office. Tony and Jeremy would work in the garden, clear up the greenhouse and generally keep things in order. Tony was also a brilliant and reliable car park attendant, always spending hours sorting out the parking during open days, project launches and the annual Apple Days.

Ian and Mary Pearce were another delightful couple who became regular volunteers at the Centre. Before they knew about INSC, Ian would ride past the top of the lane on his bike and see our sign. One day, he ventured down to visit us and, once in the gate, was hooked! He became my chief grass cutter and tool mechanic. When I started once-a-month Sunday morning gardening sessions to keep the garden under control, he and Mary would turn up and do at least two hours' work before lunch.

Ian took charge of mowing the path through the meadow and keeping the Centre's main path borders under control. One year, the directive came down from head office to say all operatives of strimmers were to wear not only protective clothing but boots, safety glasses, ear muffs and helmets. I did explain that was rather extreme, bearing in mind, in his younger days, Ian had trained during 1944 at RAF Halton, dismantled and put back aeroplane engines and had also flown Mosquitoes as part the Air Sea Rescue Squadron.

"Don't argue. Those are the rules." I was told.

"Oh, I don't think so, Sally," Ian said when I explained the situation to him. "I'm perfectly capable of using a strimmer. Anyway, I won't be able to see, with all that clobber on."

"I know that. You know that," I replied, feeling awful. "But, if you take a leg off, you won't be covered by insurance."

How insulting, I thought. Ian just smiled.

Next day, Ian was still smiling.

"Sally," he said. "I spoke to my insurers and they won't insure me because I am too old." (He was in his mid seventies). "So don't worry. I'll carry on as normal and, if I take a leg off, it's my own damn fault!"

Both Ian and Mary became personal friends. He was an incredibly kind man, who wanted to help the whole world. His politics were to the left of Mother Theresa; mine slightly right of Attila the Hun! Once a month, I would be invited for Sunday morning coffee and Mary would tolerate him and me going at it hammer and tongs, disagreeing about everything. I found the discussions stimulating. We never fell out; we begged to differ but learnt to accept that our views were opposites.

Poppy Thomas was another marvellous character. She had worked in a local day-care centre, organising and running activities, occasionally bringing her groups to the newly opened INSC to help in the garden. She knew about Iver before I turned up, as she and Ron Simpson, who managed the day centre, had also been on the committee which oversaw the creation of INSC. She was a northern lass i.e. straight forward and no-nonsense but with a heart of gold. I was introduced to her at an Iver Support Group meeting and, after organising the first outdoor Nativity at INSC, where many of the main characters were played by adults with special needs, she leaned across the row of seats and said, "Congratulations. I know what that took to put on." Over the years, we became firm friends.

At the care centre where she worked, Poppy also looked after their bees and, when it was decided to move them away, asked if Iver would like them. "Yes", I simply said. She and her husband then organised to bring the hives and bees over and she became known affectionately as 'the bee lady'. An adult special needs group helped with cleaning the hives of her beloved bees, whom she called 'my girls', by scraping the frames clean after the honey had been extracted. She was so enthusiastic about her 'girls', I often asked her to give talks about them and bee keeping in general.

Every year she would tell me we would not get any honey, and every year, I would have to hunt around for sufficient jars to hold the bees' generous harvest which would normally sell out within a fortnight! Thanks to a donation, she eventually had her own bee hut for storing all the paraphernalia needed. Poppy was also brilliant at keeping children spellbound whilst talking about bees and beeswax, especially during 'The Science of Christmas' sessions.

When she decided finally to retire and depart for pastures new, we were lucky to have the services of Penny and Ken Perry to take over care of the beehives. They did a marvellous job, for which I was truly grateful.

Ron Simpson not only helped young, physically disabled people at the day-care centre but was also involved in the creation of INSC as part of the initial Support Group committee. It was he who introduced Poppy who, at that time, was a part-time activity leader at his centre.

He was all for practicalities rather than paper, down to earth and a person who got the job done. Ron remained on the INSC Support Group for many years and was both helpful and encouraging with whatever was going on at the Centre. He was also a carol singer par excellence, when he would play the part of one of the three kings in our live Nativity tableau, held annually for several years in The Pavilions shopping centre in nearby Uxbridge.

Lyn Cradock, who helped during our early years, was our salt dough queen and a general good egg. She was always full of fun and willingly undertook all the miscellaneous jobs which helped keep the Centre running efficiently.

Henry Avery was another delightful volunteer. He was introduced to the Centre by Bill and, in time, became my part-time gardener. He had not been with us long when he asked, "Could I be a volunteer as well?"

He was a retired policeman, from the days when they patrolled our streets and knew who all the local troublemakers were–and dealt with them. In 2005, 'The Year of the Volunteer', I produced 'Memories are Made of This' [sic], a booklet which sang the praises of my own volunteers. At the end of Henry's story, I wrote: 'Henry is one of those lovable guys who never holds a grudge. Nothing seems to faze him and he is so laid-back, it is a wonder he doesn't fall over'. He had a wonderful rapport with 'The Tuesday Volunteers' and they, in turn, responded to him. He also had a flair for woodwork.

Henry would often send me postcards from where he and his wife Lynne were holidaying. One year, it was addressed to: 'The crotchety but kindly Sally'. I played hell when he returned and said, "Well you are." It was his way of telling me I was letting work get on top of me and was not giving time to the volunteers. I took the hint.

He and I were great film fans, especially westerns and we would have many discussions on the subject. One day, he came into the office and showed me a stunning wooden carving of a bronco rider.

"It's beautiful," I said, running my hand over the wood.

"I've inscribed something on the back," he said. "Do you think it's appropriate?"

Turning the piece over, I read the inscription, 'To my friend, Sal from Hen.' For once, I was speechless. I got up and gave him a kiss on his cheek. I am not sure who was the more embarrassed. "Thank you. It's …beautiful," I whispered, as he quickly got up and left the office.

After we constructed the new outdoor rainforest, housed in a polytunnel, I discovered, without asking, he had carved an exquisite plaque for the entrance.

His wife Lynne was just as gracious. Between her myriad

of other community involvements, she would always be on hand to help with catering for open days, fundraising days and project launches.

Bill Harris's wife Lily was another delightful lady. Apparently, not long before his death, Bill had said to her, "If anything happens to me, can you carry on at Iver when I leave off?"

"Yes," Lily replied. "But not in the garden!"

Despite not being a volunteer, Lily always provided raffle prizes for all occasions, many courtesy of her local shopkeepers' generosity. Each year after Bill's death, she also donated a plant in remembrance of him, for the Centre's garden.

Mary Pomeroy, a talented young artist, held weekend painting sessions for children which were popular. She helped at the Study Centre during '2001: A Space Experience', our open days and also at Apple Day by running activities for children. Every year, she created a unique 'Iver Award' which was then presented during our September anniversary lunch to those volunteers who had 'gone beyond the call of duty'.

Pat Davidson brought a special needs group to the Centre every week for years and, when she retired, came back as a volunteer, willing and able to put her hand to anything which needed doing.

Eve Abbe, a delightful Cambridge graduate from Uganda, was waiting for her work permit to come through when she arrived at the Centre. After my usual chat about Iver and our ethos, she offered to give talks on her work protecting African elephants which proved popular. She would not accept any remuneration, instead giving the money for her

71

talks to the Centre. She played a major role in establishing the Uganda Wildlife Authority and has now published two books; 'My Elephants and My People' and, for children, 'The Meeting at Got Keyo'.

Colin Hook, Hazel's husband, helped with putting up and taking down the marquee on several occasions, both at the Centre and for Apple Day in a field at Home Cottage Farm, Iver. In 1998, he played the part of Joseph at our annual carol-singing fund raising event in The Pavilions shopping centre, Uxbridge. Several years later, I 'hooked' Colin into helping create a real seashore at one end of the large pond which we then used during the 'Sea and Seashore' activity for school and other groups.

And even more volunteers

Over the years, a small army of people would give their services voluntarily but it would be impossible to mention every person who gave their time over the eighteen years I was manager. Here are some:

Geoff Fielding would bring in his boa constrictor and other snakes then stand for hours during open days showing visitors how to hold them.

Woodturner, Alan Spargo, like Geoff Fielding, would spend his day demonstrating his craft, much to the fascination of on-lookers. He gave his donations to the Centre.

Mary Furnell not only demonstrated spinning and weaving techniques; she was also marvellous at making corn dollies.

Muriel Caley had a tremendous artistic gift which contributed to the early 'Experiences'.

Elizabeth Whiting, like Ron Simpson and Poppy Thomas, was part of the original Support Group behind the creation of INSC and went on to be one of my catering team for launches, events and 'Experiences'. She was a lovely, charming, elegant lady who supported me in everything.

Dianne Prutton arrived at the beginning of Iver's development. In our first live Nativity, in Uxbridge shopping centre, she played one of the kings. She proved brilliant in the garden, was so hard-working, pleasant and a joy to have around. Her gardening talents were recognised when she went on to become Head Gardener at a wonderful, late medieval manor house.

Carolyn [Elliott] Barton-Hide was one of my early volunteers who came along on Tuesdays to help in the garden. In 'The Countryside Game', she helped clear the small pond of organic debris along with tackling the copious growth of weeds. When we built the raised-bed pond in front of the log cabin, she helped by laying some of the bricks, the proof being her initials carved in the cement!

From head office at Denham, I had wonderful encouragement from Pat Garrard, Gerry Alexander, Clare Bill, Lorraine Jones and Jackie Talbot, all of whom, not only supported the Centre 'officially', but also gave their time in a voluntary capacity at various events.

From the day I started at the Centre, Gerry was both supportive and encouraging. She also kept her promise, after retiring from head office, of sorting out and collating the official figures i.e. volunteers, visitors and activists; the last being those who attended events. These statistics were needed for the monthly report I was required to send to head office.

Clare Bill, as well as being the Accounts Assistant at Groundwork Thames Valley, somehow found time to help at many of our INSC events. She was usually to be glimpsed bustling about doing the essential little things which make everything go like clockwork and was a tireless supporter of all things Iver.

Clare Bill's husband Stan was a tremendous help when I needed both large and lesser amounts of printing done but had little budget left. 'The Reading Scheme' was a case in point when the firm he worked for offered to print the small number of books, written by the children, without charge. During our open days or other public events, Stan would often lend a hand to help Clare with her teddy tombola stall or wherever else he was needed.

Jill Nicholas occasionally helped with 'I'm Bored' craft sessions and latterly ran children's parties, with environmental themes, on Saturday afternoons, always leaving the place clean and tidy afterwards.

Liz Pinfold helped out occasionally with weeding and, in particular, tackled much of the overgrowth in 'The Countryside Game' area. She also worked in the background during our 2005 'In the Mood' dinner and dance and assisted at one of our summer holiday 'I'm Bored' children's week.

Suzanne [Payne] Macaree, an occasional volunteer in the garden, came to the rescue when we were a king short for one of the fundraising live Christmas Nativities in Uxbridge. A true supporter of Iver, she attended both dinner and dance evenings and regularly came along to our open days.

The Pearson family was very supportive. As youngsters, Joanna and Ben were looked after by neighbour Kareth during school holidays and often after school. They soon became regular junior volunteers at the Centre. They were always regaling their parents about the fun and occasional responsibilities they had at 'work'. I am not a computer person and after the children mentioned to Ian, their father, who had a computer business, the problems I was having, he offered to help design Iver's initial web site, a job which, once it was complete, made all the difference to getting our name out there. His wife Jenny also did a wonderful job, dressed in a WRAF uniform at the 'Dig for Victory' fund raising dinner, helping serve guests then clearing up the debris afterwards.

Bunty King, National Grid graduate George's[2] delightful mother, gave up her Sundays when we held the gardening sessions to keep the various gardens under control. A lady who was full of life and laughter; a typical 'Iverite'!

Burt George was an interesting odd-job man, putting his hand to gardening and anything else which needed doing. He was a great supporter of the Royal British Legion, having served in the army, and came dressed for the occasion, along with the RBL Standard for the Iver area, to the children's tea party which we held during 'Dig for Victory'. He also introduced his wife to the Study Centre.

Ena George, Burt's wife, was a delightful lady who could be relied upon and who fitted in with my team, always there when an extra pair of hands was required.

June Mitchell, a marvellous general helper, won the INSC Most Promising Newcomer award in 2012.

---

2   You can read about George in Chapter Seven: 'The National Grid Graduate Scheme'

Jim Gore, who came to the Centre in later years, proved to be a great help in the garden.

Anne Smith, a lovely, vibrant lady, gave her time and talents to help in the garden and do anything else which was required. She also encouraged the company she worked for to sponsor many of our projects.

Julie Rowlands joined towards the end of my time at INSC and did an excellent job helping to run visits from schools and our special needs groups.

David Windaybank, a delightful gentleman, worked with Geoff in the garden where he proved to be a terrific asset.

Jane Axworthy, my sister and wife of David[3], often helped with groups during school holidays. At Christmas, along with a merry choir of volunteers, each of us in costume, she joined us for our fund-raising carols appearance in The Pavilions shopping centre in Uxbridge. One year she was a shepherd and, on another, played the part of Mary, even having a real baby to hold, courtesy of a family member.

Jay Allison volunteered in the early days of Iver and I remember her as always willing and able to take on any necessary jobs to keep the place running smoothly. There was always laughter and enthusiasm when she was around.

Ian Hutchby was a great help during our many school and group visits.

Gina Martin used her talents to create a huge willow-woven frog structure which was placed on the 'Get down to Nature' assault course where visiting children loved running through it.

---

3   You can read about David in the story of our outdoor Nativity at the Study Centre in Chapter Five: 'Extras'

Asha Kamboj was one of my last volunteers before I left and was with me for about a year. She put her hand towards everything which needed doing – except cleaning the toilet! Apparently, I was quite adamant that she was not to do this; it was my prerogative! We now meet once a year for lunch and have a wonderful time catching up on what each of us has been doing, discussing life in general and, of course, putting the world to rights!

The following also deserve a mention as they became typical 'Iverites' – hard-working and reliable, in that they always made themselves available when called upon to help out in the garden, with visiting groups or wherever their strengths lay: Neil Dancer, Juliette Green, Jan Wright, David Reynolds, Angie Parlow, Paul Brennan, Jean Phillips, Cherry Hammond, Ann Mathers, Janet Symes and Roger Ferrin.

And last, but certainly not least, a very special person was Nicholas Smith, the community liaison person for a well-known bank. He had a budget for helping small, local charities and, after seeing first-hand what we were doing, was tremendously supportive over the years I was at Iver and constantly looking for funding for our many projects. He willingly organised quiz nights, match-funding the takings. He sponsored one of our 'firm's outings' and a volunteers' dinner. One summer, as a guest at our annual volunteers' lunch, I took the opportunity to ask him if he would hand out the 'Iver Awards' which were given to those volunteers who were outstanding in what they had done that year for INSC. He also organised the extremely popular Christmas present wrapping sessions, held in the local shopping centre. When I, plus any volunteers who could spare an hour or more, helped, a percentage of the takings was allocated to Iver. I still remember the hours I spent in the shopping centre doing Christmas gift wrapping and, on one Christmas Eve, not getting home until 7.30 pm!

When I had the idea to hold our 'In the Mood' dinner and dance in 2005, Nicholas's budget helped with the funding. He also helped with funding in September 2015 for Iver's twenty-fifth anniversary afternoon tea which was held at the Centre. It was attended by many of my staff and volunteers, all of whom enjoyed renewing acquaintances, chatting and reminiscing about the fun times we all had together over the years.

While I was writing about my volunteers, I contacted Nicholas to ask if I had missed anything out. I certainly had. I had forgotten he also helped manually at the Centre. His volunteering included: helping create the seashore at one end of the big pond, moving several huge, heavy, bags of ballast and assisting with laying the foundation then erection, of a workshop, with the help of the US Navy! He carried out repairs to the rainforest polytunnel. Along with a regional director using his chainsaw, the pair of them cut up dozens of logs and, lastly, he helped erect a fence. Nicholas was a gentleman with a heart of gold who supported us unreservedly.

*

During the summer of my first year at INSC, I held a volunteers' lunch for my team of five.

A few years after I started, I wanted to show how much I appreciated what my volunteers gave INSC. In August 1996, after our annual volunteers' lunch, the 'Ivers', our equivalent of the Oscars, were initiated, with awards for categories such as: Volunteer of the Year, Best Individual Achievement, Most Promising Newcomer, Best Original Idea and The Merrill-Hinson Award, the last being given to the most obstinate, disobedient and awkward volunteer and was named after the two volunteers whose surnames instigated it!

In my last year at the Centre, it gave me the greatest pleasure to welcome the fifty-nine volunteers who joined me on that final, special day. We spent a memorable afternoon enjoying good food while recalling our many happy times together.

Over the course of my years as manager, I came to realise Iver had practically become the volunteers' second home; a place where friendships were formed and troubles often shared.

*

Christmas at the Centre was always special. Initially, a dozen or so of us went out to a local restaurant but, when the volunteer numbers soared, it was decided to hold a more informal Christmas dinner at the Centre, do our own catering, occasionally supplemented by using a local take-away delivery service. We also provided our own entertainment. We would all cram into the larger activity room for a riotous dinner and, each year, Henry lived his dream, becoming the stand-up comedian for the evening.

*

During the year, I would organise outings, many of which the volunteers willingly paid for themselves. Places we visited included the Hampton Court Flower Show, Duxford Museum and Highgrove House. We crossed the Channel three times to visit Restaurant du Cap, a superb fish restaurant on the French coast at Escalles after, of course, spending a fortune at the supermarket in Calais. On the third occasion, we even managed to visit Boulogne as well. During each visit, we always managed a paddle in the sea before returning on Le Shuttle and once, by boat.

These were heady days and why it worked was simple.

The volunteers cared about each other, cared about the people who came to the Centre and, most importantly, took responsibility. They put in hours of their time and not once did they ever let me down. If they said they would do

The beach at Escalles, France
©Kareth Paterson

something, they did. I, in turn, cared about them. They were my second family and I would like to think I never let them down and am sure they would have told me if I had– as Henry did! We communicated with each other, helped each other, worked hard, laughed an awful lot, occasionally cried but, most of all, we quietly took pride in our achievements and successes, and we enjoyed ourselves.

The Ladies in the Office

I was not only blessed with volunteer support over the years but also with the ladies who were my secretaries and looked after the office. They were paid a small wage but, like the volunteers, gave me their commitment, incredible efficiency, enthusiasm, laughter and hard work. They also gave lots of volunteer time. Funnily enough, their names all began with a 'J' – Judith, Jill, Jackie and Jan.

Judith Hammond, who I first met when she worked at head office in Denham, after leaving, joined me at INSC and was very supportive during my early years. Jill Myers was renowned for her sausage plaits which were a mainstay for almost all catered events. Jackie Naughton used her artistic talents face painting at our Open Days and on Apple Day. Jan Gosling I will always remember for her chocolate bars, despite me telling her not to keep bringing them in! I admit it here and now; chocolate is my downfall!

When I was preparing to retire, to help out the next manager, I created a folder of how the place was run, purely for information. I then asked Jan to list what she did. There were forty-two items on her list!

THREE
VOLUNTEERS' THOUGHTS

AND SOME COMMENTS OF MY OWN.

What did the volunteers get out of Iver? As the manager, a local newspaper asked me for an article about my volunteer group. I decided to write to them all, asking for their (printable!) opinions of why they volunteered at Iver and what they got out of it.

Here are a few of the replies I received, followed by my own thoughts on that person.

Peter Hinson wrote:

I am fortunate to have a creative ability which I am pleased to offer to the Study Centre – the reward is being in a position to volunteer this service and to enjoy the 'esprit de corps' of the many other helpers.

Peter's artistic talent was quite extraordinary and, having run his own display company, he knew how to get round every problem when we were creating and building the 'Experiences' and my many other requests as well. When I set up Sunday morning weeding sessions to keep the place under control, Peter, not a 'weeding' person, would happily spend time in the kitchen making lunch for when we had had enough and needed some refreshments. In a nutshell, Peter was artistic, generous and clever. We could not have achieved what we did without his input.

Gwen, Peter's wife wrote:

When we stumbled across Iver Nature Study Centre in October 1994, we had no idea of the integral part it was to play in our immediate future.

My husband, Peter became involved in projects proposed at that time which was good for him because he was starting to retire from his main work in exhibitions, seminars etc which he designed, constructed and installed. All was jogging along fine, then our elder daughter was diagnosed with breast cancer, just three weeks before her second little boy was due to be born. That was in May 1995 and so began the hardest time in our lives.

Peter continued to be involved with projects at the Centre and these gave us a focus which then enabled us to cope with such difficulty and sadness. Our daughter passed away in 1997 when her firstborn son, Jamie, was five-and-a-half and her younger son, Ben, not quite two years old. During all this time, we used to take the children down to the Centre for birthday parties – Ben had his second birthday there, as did his older brother, Jamie, with his friends, for the following years and they enjoyed all the organised activities.

Our time there brought to us a group of really lovely people, many of whom we are still in contact with. Peter continued to work with Sally and her crew for many years, until she retired in 2009.

Gwen's story is just one example of how Iver Nature Study Centre and my volunteers helped one family through a difficult time.

She turned up for all our events, helping wherever necessary. As well as being a marvellous 'clearer upper' after events, and a general supporter, she was also a great spell checker.

Ian Pearce's contribution was:

I went to Iver originally because I liked the idea behind the whole project. I'm still here because life would seem empty without it and without the company of a broad mix of non-conformist, enthusiastic staff and volunteers. Also, because I would hate to miss out on what's round the next corner!

Mary, his wife, wrote:

I like the feeling of belonging to a team where everyone enjoys the challenges which Sally thinks up. There is always something planned and, when you look at past successes – '2001: A Space Experience', 'The Garden of Time', 'The Olive Grove', 'Africa' etc., it is good to feel you were part of these projects. And, of course, being a member of 'The Apple Tarts' line dancing team!

Ian and Mary were an extraordinary couple. They became involved with catering, gardening and non-artistic jobs. It was not just at Iver they volunteered. They also helped out with the local Parkinson's disease group and a stroke club.

About a year after Peter and Gwen joined the volunteer team, their eldest daughter, Kate, tragically died from cancer. Sometime later, their son-in-law, Mick, asked if I would like to join him for the London to Brighton cycle ride, to raise funds for a cancer charity, to which I readily agreed. At the end of the race, to my surprise, both Ian and Mary were standing just before the finishing line, calling out to get my attention and holding aloft a glass of gin and tonic – which I readily drank before crossing the line! They had driven all the way to Brighton to support our efforts. We all ended up on the beach eating fish and chips. Despite the agonies and exhaustion remembered from my first long-distance cycle ride, I challenged myself and completed a second the following year.

Sue Taylor's quote,

Lending a hand at Iver is a worthwhile activity and one always comes away feeling better for having been there.

Sue loved using her creative talent at the Centre and would often give her time and talent in helping others during the 'Experiences' when they came up against a problem. I got to know how she worked. I would say what I wanted then leave her to her own devices. Near lunch, or teatime, I would go to where she was working and she would spend ten or fifteen minutes telling me what she had done. It was usually brilliant. I would say so and she was satisfied. She just needed encouragement.

Henry Avery wrote:

> I was introduced by another volunteer. I was not sure at first if the Centre was quite my scene but was quickly swept along by the enthusiasm and comradeship of the other members of staff. I now get more from the Centre than I put into it which says much for the INSC spirit.

At the Iver Christmas dinners, Henry realised his ambition of being not only a stand-up comedian but also a cabaret act, teller of silly stories and, on one never-to-be-forgotten occasion, being the better half of a duet we sang together, much to everyone's amusement.

Lynne, Henry's wife added:

> I attended an Open Day at Iver and was so impressed by the attitude and enthusiasm of the staff and volunteers who work there, that I felt I should like to be part of the team.

Reliable and supportive are the first two words which come to mind when I think of Lynne. When we put on events, she became our chief cook and bottle washer, handling all catering with a smile. She was a real 'down to earth' person who just got on with things.

Poppy Thomas's thoughts:

I wrote down a long list, starting with the manager's threat of thumb screws and the evil eye, down to my feelings after I have spent some time at the Centre and it all boils down to my being valued by you, your staff and the other vols.

Poppy was quite extraordinary with her time and talents. She would help out with school visits, undertake talks on bee keeping and was always there helping with the catering for open days, project launches and gardening.

Kareth Paterson wrote:

I volunteer at Iver because, no matter how small or large a contribution, it is always appreciated. It is like one's family – always encouraging, never critical.

Kareth turned her hand to almost everything which went on at Iver. She instigated a monthly stroll around the various gardens, studied courses in alternative therapies, using our National Grid graduate, Susi[4] and me as guinea pigs, always helped out with school visits on every subject and at every holiday play scheme. She was also looking after two children, Joanna and Ben, during the school holidays and after school, frequently bringing them to the Centre. They soon became very keen volunteers themselves, helping in the garden, during the 'I'm Bored' summer week and both preparing and clearing up materials for activities.

Hazel Hook wrote:

---

4   You can read more about Susi in Chapter Seven

The success of INSC is due almost entirely to Sally with the support of her staff. Her immense enthusiasm and boundless energy, with limited funds and resources, is so infectious that any task undertaken usually proves so satisfying that we return for another dose. It is with Sally's powers of persuasion, cajoling or simply press-ganging her volunteers into submission that so much has been achieved.

In fact, to coin a phrase 'so much is owed by so many to so few' applies mainly to Sally's team. INSC goes from strength to strength and just has to be seen to be believed. Long may it continue.

Hazel was part of the education and catering team and a delightful volunteer, constantly smiling and willing to put her hand to anything. Always thoughtful. On one occasion, without being asked, much needed sustenance in the way of tea/coffee and nibbles appeared whilst we were erecting the marquee in the orchard for Apple Day!

Bill Harris's quote:

Gardening is a hobby I enjoy very much, and it helps some disabled people and school children learn about how the food they eat is grown. I also find this is relaxing, and working with various disabled groups and school children is a worthwhile pastime. If I was not involved in this activity, as a pensioner, I would be sitting at home rather fed up.

Bill was a gentle, thoughtful soul who took 'The Tuesday

Volunteers', who were a special needs group, under his wing. They did a great job keeping the vegetable patch under control which became a good teaching aid.

Vic and Jan Merrill wrote:

How did we get enmeshed in the first place? The answer is that we don't know. In our case, we naively stopped at INSC after getting some eggs from the farm to see some sort of event they were advertising ('The Rainforest Experience') – fatal. We haven't found an escape route yet. We suspect it is something they put in the tea, following the query on arrival, "Haven't you got tea? Hang on, I'll get you one." Everyone at Iver makes you feel wanted; perhaps that's their secret.

I remember Vic and Jan coming to the Study Centre one Saturday morning and being 'grilled' by them as to what exactly we were doing. Having stumbled my way through the answers, they then offered to bring their pythons along! That was the beginning of a wonderful period for Iver.

On one memorable occasion, I phoned with only an hour before the arrival of an expected visiting group because I had forgotten to book them, but they turned up, without rancour or a murmur.

When something needed fixing, Vic would be there, with his analytical brain to work out the problem. They are one of the kindest couples I have had the pleasure of knowing.

Gill Kerr wrote:

At Iver, Sally and her staff have combined niceness with

competence. They are good at saying thanks and there is a high level of friendship between volunteers and staff. Sally is also good at identifying talent. Iver also shows that disability is not preclusion to volunteering. Disabled and able-bodied volunteers can all work together – and both groups benefit from the experience.

Gill used her time as an Iver volunteer to produce a dissertation as part of her final year studies for a BSc (Hons) in Management Studies at Brunel University. A few years on, she returned to help at our Saturday morning 'Once upon a Time' reading scheme by making hot drinks for the adults, juice for the children then tidying up at the end of each session.

*

After I retired, I asked some of the volunteers from my final years for their thoughts of how they had seen INSC.

Lily Harris declared:

I made lots of friends. We all just seemed to get on.'

Lily kept her promise to Bill and, after he died, became a volunteer at the Centre. She proved to be a great asset as a stalwart of our marvellous catering team. She also continued to provide raffle prizes for all occasions, many courtesy of her local shopkeepers' generosity, with whom she continued to have a great rapport.

Chris Hare's quote:

It was just being part of something where everyone was so friendly and produced wonderful things!

Chris was introduced to the Centre by Lily. She was brilliant at needle craft and all catering needs.

Keith and his wife Jean, by this time, had moved to Wiltshire and unfortunately, were unable to come to my leaving do in February 2009. However, he sent a letter which included the following:

...I have fond memories of working at INSC for many years. Sally rescued me from the trough of despondency at being made redundant when I joined, shortly after her arrival, as a general handyman. 'When you've got a minute, Keith' was her usual greeting and I never had an idle moment all the time I was there.

'This is the last major project' was her annual promise when I was involved in some major construction exercise! I was sorry to say goodbye to INSC when Jean and I moved from the area.

Jean, his wife, was an expert gardener who brought her talents to the Study Centre by creating our scented garden.

During my first autumn, a young lady, called Kerstin Schrottke, appeared on the doorstep who, much to my surprise, hailed from Germany! She was my one and only full-time volunteer and spent twelve months with us. After contacting her to ask if she would like to write something about her year at Iver, she kindly found the time to send the following:

My little story of the Iver Nature Study Centre began almost thirty years ago, when I was a nineteen-year-old German pupil with the vision of doing something useful for nature, between school and study. Looking for offers of a voluntary position in environmental organisations, I received a very kind invitation from the Kent Thames-side Groundwork Trust in England. In early September 1991, when I left Germany for my 'voluntary ecological' year, I was unaware the most impressive twelve months were about to start, working for a wonderful, unique project.

After arriving in Dartford, I found the Trust was in a very busy organising phase and consequently, I was promised I would have more benefit by being involved in the work of the Colne Valley Park Groundwork Trust in Denham and in particular, their Iver Nature Study Centre. I still thank the Trust's team for the chance they provided, by relocating my one year to become the first full-time volunteer at Iver.

In the Centre's flyer which I was given at the Trust's head office, Iver was nicely described; the little wooden cabin on the 1.5-acre site with its old cottage garden recreated into different but typically British habitats. In particular, I was deeply impressed by the fact that the facility was created to meet the needs of people with disabilities. I had not seen such an approach of dealing with the sensitising of human beings for nature and nature conservation on one hand and, on the other, including an important social element by involving people with special needs.

Soon after my first working days, I realised the flyer

provided only a tiny overview of the large variety of activities the visitors could experience at the Centre day by day. Nature was discovered in different visitor–adapted ways, either by observing, exploring, learning, working or playing. They could also relax in the outdoor area or participate in the various indoor activities, based around special nature-related event days and weeks.

Visitors, whether young, old, healthy, disabled, alone or in groups came together and often quickly socialised in a wonderful, life-enhancing manner. For me, it was the first time I had worked with less-able people and I learned a lot about them and even more important, from them.

From my very first day onwards, I felt an extremely pleasant life force, a vitality which was in fact, the Centre's manager – Sally Munn. In my opinion, it is no exaggeration to write that she was the Centre. Every day, she gave life to it all. She was full of ideas, plans and visions – inspiring those around her in a unique way and using her talent of communicating most productively. The Centre developed to become a place where many people enjoyed their time and supported it in a very non-bureaucratic, most charming way. Volunteers of different ages and backgrounds also came to help in extraordinary ways and made Iver a wonderful place to meet. It was due to Sally that the Centre quickly grew to become a very successful, much used, well-known place.

My one year at the Centre passed by very fast, fully packed with new impressions, experiences and a wonderful, everlasting friendship. Even after thirty years, I am still happy and grateful to have been part of a fabulous place for that year when I met people willing to support nature and social related projects so selflessly. My year at Iver was eye-opening in a way, realising everyone can do something to make our living atmosphere a bit better. We do not have to wait for changes; we can work for them, each within their own capability, with or without disabilities.

Kerstin was a pleasure to have around, full of good ideas and always up for a challenge when I needed help with getting the Centre up and running.

When I asked Geoff Thomas, who turned his hand to most things, for his views, he had this to say:

I first started working at INSC when I was in my fifties, after my job had been made redundant. I had worked in the printing, design and graphic sector, having completed my apprenticeship following school. With the emergence of new technology and being of a certain age, I was encountering difficulties in finding suitable work.

'At the INSC I was given challenging projects to design and construct. It's not often you get asked to build a sixteen-foot high space shuttle and a Mission Control! My involvement in all the projects was instrumental in re-building my self-worth and sense of being valued. Importantly also, I met many inspiring and interesting individuals who willingly gave their time and skills to INSC in a volunteering capacity. The friendships I made were wonderful and have been long-lasting. I feel my life was enriched during the years I spent there.

Looking back, I asked Geoff to do some phenomenal things and he always came up trumps. I knew he had tremendous artistic talent, was an accomplished gardener and brilliant at construction. He willingly gave his time and expertise to support the Centre.

Hazel said:

It is a privilege to be connected, albeit in only a very small way, with a group of people who care so much for others, particularly those less fortunate. Their care and interest in the environment is unbounded which they succeed in passing on to so many, both young and not so young. We never cease to be amazed how much is 'produced' from a comparatively small site – every square inch is put to such good use.

I remember Hazel as a delightful person, so warm and fun-loving, always laughing whenever she was asked to do something.

Shelagh Patmore came to the Centre in 2006. She said:

Having just retired, I was looking for something to keep my body fit and mind active as well as being enjoyable. Becoming a volunteer at INSC met these requirements. I derived a great deal of satisfaction and enjoyment as a volunteer at the Centre and have many happy memories of my time there. Working with the other volunteers was a pleasure. They were conscientious, hard-working and great fun to be with.

'The planning and organisation by Sally enabled

special-needs and educational activities to take place in a safe and well-run environment. Showing the school parties round the various areas of the Centre, in order for them to learn about different environments, watching their excitement and enjoyment of 'hands-on' activities, I found very rewarding. Their comments, questions and answers to questions, some of which were very amusing, were a delight. Happy days.

She was a fantastic asset to the Centre, both working in the garden and helping run visiting groups. In her early days, long before coming to Iver, she ran a small nursery for young children from her home, with help from her mother. One day, she mentioned a teacher at the local school had commented to her, 'we can always tell if the child has been to you. When they start school, they can write their name, go to the toilet on their own, put on their coat and sit down at a table to have their meal'. She was so encouraging and patient with the children who came to the Centre, they responded well to her.

Jan Gosling, who ran the office, had this to say:

My time working at the Iver Nature Study Centre was a happy one.

I have fond memories of a woman with so much energy and enthusiasm. The first time I met Sally, I thought, 'this woman is a doer' and she was. If anything needed doing, you could be sure Sally found a person or a way to do it.

The Centre was a warm, welcoming place, a sanctuary for many away from the hustle and bustle of the demanding lives we have. Even though it was a busy and popular place, there always seemed a peace to it.

I loved working there and being able to wander through the gardens and chat to the volunteers, and I loved seeing the children's faces when they were doing events such as candle rolling or playing on the assault course.

The Centre and Sally were one and the same for years but, when it was time for Sally to retire, I decided it was time for me to move on and we left the Centre together in 2009.

A lot of friendships were formed at Iver Nature Study Centre, and it is a great testament to Sally that she has kept in touch with nearly all the volunteers and employees who were with her during her time there.

Jan was a delight to have in the office. Not only was she efficient, she could also handle everything, without me having to tell her what needed doing! There was always a lot of laughter when she was around!

When I asked Roy Shepard for his views he said:

I was astounded when you burst upon my rather staid and ring-fenced life. I was sitting in the main office at the Groundwork premises, assisting with clerical work and photo copying. You whizzed in and whizzed out and, in-between, did what you needed to do.

At some point after this, I was asked if I would like to go and help at Iver (around October 2001). I was picked up by you and Monique and was in a very defensive mood. However, I quickly found the place fascinating and the various folk who were involved a delight.

The Centre did so much. It was like being in a buoyant place of multi-faceted interest and inspiration. The people who benefited were of all ages and abilities, and they just loved the place.

Roy was great fun to have as a volunteer, mainly because he was a great raconteur. He worked in the garden, often with Geoff, and became known as 'the teasel man' because, one day, I had left the office feeling rather fatigued (to put it politely!), to have a walk around the garden and came across him uprooting a beautiful teasel which must have had at least twenty heads on it.

"What the hell are you doing?" I shouted, rather ungraciously.

He just stood there, holding the gigantic, spiky plant in one hand, garden fork in the other, looking rather perplexed! Needless to say, I apologised and we laughed. He must have forgiven me because, together with Geoff and his wife Rosemary, we still meet monthly to have lunch together.

And finally, Iver's youngest volunteers.

Ben Pearson became our youngest volunteer, 'recruited' at the age of three when Kareth took on childminding her next door neighbours' two children. From his first visit in December 1999, he fitted in and, within weeks, was 'working' with Henry and 'The Tuesday Volunteers' in the vegetable plot.

On one memorable occasion, aged four, having 'helped' the men building the *Iverana* space shuttle, after being told to be on his best behaviour, Ben reappeared several hours later, grinning from ear to ear but with trousers and anorak covered in splashes of white paint! Jumping up and down with excitement, he said to me, "I helped a lot but I only painted a little." Kareth can still recall having spent that evening scrubbing, rubbing and rinsing his clothes clean, then keeping her heating on all night to dry everything so his parents would never know. Well, they will after reading this!

He was willing to do anything asked of him and, by the age of ten, during school holidays, as well as helping clean the cabin, washing dishes, paint pots and brushes, he occasionally manned my office, answering the telephone or greeting visitors when I was called away to a different part of the Centre.

Ben was a typical boy, running around, getting away with not doing much but always, in the end, helping where necessary! He had a wicked sense of humour and thought it hilarious when he first soaked me with water after the end of one summer's 'I'm Bored' week (more of that later) which went on to become a yearly tradition. He originally denied his involvement but, unfortunately for him, there is a photograph of him holding the still-dripping hose!

Joanna (Jo), Ben's older sister, like him, came along to every 'I'm Bored' holiday scheme from 1999 to 2006, initially as a participant but, as the years passed, took on the role of Group Leader. Like her brother, she did everything asked of her and became a real asset around the place during the school holidays. She was an expert pencil sharpener, paint pot/brushes cleaner and dishes and floor washer-upper. On several occasions, she took work home, e.g. cutting out shapes for collages or sugar paper frogs. Nothing was too much for her and, like the adult volunteers, when she said she would do something, she did.

In 2005, she became the youngest ever recipient of our prestigious Volunteer of the Year Award. When interviewed for a local paper, she said,

> I get so much enjoyment out of everything. Now I am old enough to help younger children get the same value out of the experience of coming here as I do.

Now known as Jo, she has grown into a delightful lady who, after several years as a medical secretary in the private sector, is now director of her own medical secretarial business.

Jo and Ben were a pleasure to have around and, unlike some children of the same ages, were articulate, enthusiastic, reliable and had both the dexterity and sense to use scissors and equipment safely.

*

Looking back over my years at the Study Centre, the comments I wrote for our 'Memories are Made of This' [sic] book in 2005 still stand today.

The Iver volunteers were unique and the most talented group of people I have had the pleasure of knowing and working with. They were like an extended family in the way they supported each other and took pride in everything they did on behalf of the Centre. Every single person was very, very professional and the time each one put in for others was incalculable. I was extraordinarily lucky to have had their help, advice and friendship during my eighteen years as manager.

Now, in 2021, several volunteers have passed away and I can truthfully say, when this happens, a part of me goes with them. Although I left the Centre just over twelve years ago, I regularly think of them all.

When a few of us meet weekly in someone's home to have a meal, play cards and generally put the world to rights, the 'good old days at Iver' frequently come into the conversation. Sadly, already in this group, Peter and Lily 'Last Card Lil' are no longer with us.

I had eighteen wonderful years of support and enthusiasm from a team of people whose like I will never again experience. It was indeed a privilege and pleasure to have known them all.

FOUR

MY TWELVE YEARS AS A ~~SLAVE~~ VOLUNTEER

VOLUNTEER KARETH PATERSON'S SIDE OF THINGS.

Listed by number as a reminder of the many dozens of times we sang 'The Twelve Days of Christmas' over the years when schools or groups took part in December's 'The Science of Christmas' activities.

12 = years as one of Sally's merry band of volunteers, fleetingly as a gardener before being press-ganged into the 'eddukashun' team.

11 = assorted activities for children, to be created, adapted, tested, then enjoyed by everyone who took part.

10 = years of fund-raising for much-needed equipment and necessities.

9 = years of preventing Sally's stress levels from going through the roof by giving her a variety of natural therapy treatments.

8 = years of helping at 'I'm Bored' summer week and all the other school holiday activities.

7 = days with Sally, exploring Washington DC in 2000, which included visiting the NASA education offices for ideas to use for '2001; A Space Experience'.

6 = years of courses at colleges, studying the intricacies of basic computing, teaching, gaining an NVQ2 qualification in caring for the environment, qualifying as a complementary therapist then as a tutor, holding down two part-time weekend jobs, child-minding and fitting in volunteering at INSC. Ask a busy woman!

5 +100 = 105 three-course meals to help organise, prepare, cook and serve for the 'In the Mood' dinner and dance during 'Dig for Victory' in 2005'.

4 = awards for volunteering, plus numerous accolades and mentions in the local papers, every one of which was special as well as being unexpected.

3 = outings, dressed as one of the Three Wise Men when singing Christmas carols in The Pavilions shopping centre in Uxbridge.

2 = away-days in France for duty-free shopping, deliciously long and decadent lunches, followed by paddling on a sunny, warm, sandy beach.

...And creating a Christmas pudding recipe, suitable for school children and groups to make during their 'The Science of Christmas' visit.

FIVE
EXTRAS

AN OVERVIEW OF SOME OF OUR ACTIVITIES.

The assault course. Special schools and a special memory. The Iver Nativity. Apple Day. Our millennium project. Our millennium calendar. The Reading Scheme.

Throughout the first year of working at Iver, I was mainly concerned with providing basic natural history (not environmental in those days) activities which would attract visitors to the Centre. It was not the easiest place to get to by public transport but I thought, if we had a mini bus, we could collect small groups who would benefit from spending time in a quiet, safe, natural environment.

To catch attention, I decided to raise money towards

getting our own mini-bus by doing a charity fund-raising parachute jump with the Red Devils. Having landed safe and sound, I wrote to the Lord's Taverners charity which agreed to help. In June 1998, a thirteen-seater mini-bus was presented to the Study Centre by Judith Chalmers OBE, President of the Lady Taverners, on behalf of the Lord's Taverners, when she kindly handed over the keys to a beautiful, bright green mini-bus. It was a great addition to the Centre; we could collect 'The Tuesday Volunteers' each week and give lifts to special needs groups and school parties who needed help with transport.

The Assault Course

When we started to offer varying educational packages, such as 'Frog Week' and 'The Environment', schools began to book visits and I felt we needed a place where the children could run around in safety before we sat down to have lunch. There was a car park in front of the visitors' cabin and, in the early days, while the children had a run-around, an adult was stationed by the entrance gate to give warning of any vehicles needing access.

In 1994, I asked National Grid if we could have the unused piece of land at the back of 'The Secret Garden'. They graciously agreed and here we created our 'Get down to Nature' mini assault course which was intended to show how animals move. Time permitting, the children could go round the course three times. Adults were staged at each item to offer help and to keep an eye out for any miscreants. The children lined up by the entrance gate then, one at a time, except for the maze, were told: '...and wait for the person in front to get off before you get on…' then off they would go.

The first obstacle was 'the beetle': a narrow plank, about a foot from the ground, along which each child balanced. Second was 'the spider's web': a square, wooden structure, criss-crossed with rope which had a hole in the middle through which the child stepped without disturbing the strings of the web.

On to 'the caterpillar crawl': a rickety bridge, superbly made by Mike McTyre, from the American Scout Group 402, with the support of his father, neither of whom would accept any payment for the materials used.

Next came 'the mole hole': a wide, unused, cable pipe, donated by National Grid, through which, at ground level, the child would crawl before climbing up a little ladder attached to a pipe wall then emerge on to a small, wooden

Jo and Ben using 'the beetle' and 'the spider's web'.
©Kareth Paterson

platform. From this they jumped down to ground level before heading to 'the squirrel scramble'. Here they climbed up thick rope netting, stood on the platform at the top then, with arms open, flew off like a bird, landing in the sandy patch below. There was always a helping hand offered to the more reluctant fliers.

On one occasion, when I was overseeing this piece of equipment, a young girl, obviously somewhat nervous said, "I can't do it. I can't do it."

I replied, "You can do it. I'll hold both your hands when you jump off. Remember to bend your knees to soften your landing."

On her second round, I said, "Shall we try with me holding just one hand?"

When she stood on the platform for her final jump, she did it on her own.

For the next obstacle, Georgina King, or George, as she was known, had planted box hedging in the form of a short maze as her project whilst on the National Grid Graduate Scheme (more of which later). This mini-maze became 'the amazing-ant-antics'. Here, the children scurried along the twists and turns between hedges, trying to avoid dead ends, in their hurry to reach the exit. Right from the beginning, it proved very popular. As the years passed, the bushes grew higher and higher and, of course, the children began to get lost in it, much to their enjoyment, from the laughter and cries being heard as they negotiated their way round. By the time I departed, the hedges were over five feet high.

After emerging from the maze, the children became rabbits in a burrow by crawling through a camouflaged plastic play tunnel, courtesy of a fund-raising initiative by Kareth, then ran up to and around the totem pole, a relic from 'The Native American Indians Experience', created and constructed by Keith.

Peter Hill from National Grid was very supportive of

Thank-you letter from Annabel

everything we did at the Centre. For the assault course, as well as providing the muscle power to move the totem pole into place, he also gave us the cable pipe which became 'the mole hole'.

When Peter moved on to pastures new, Terry Smith took over his role and proved to be just as supportive of all things Iver.

After going around the totem pole, the children then ran up the little hill to 'the dormouse-dangle' which was a short length of parallel bars, built by Geoff. After crossing this hand over hand, they then ran to the far side of the hill and the final piece of equipment: a giant slide, down which they slithered like a snake.

Needless to say, the children adored doing the 'a salt course'!

Special Schools and a Special Memory

Special schools would come regularly to take part in activities. These, by and large, consisted of a class of up to ten children with two adults: the teacher and the teacher's assistant. Both were always superb with the children and we usually got through a visit in around forty minutes, without too much trouble.

One of the most memorable occasions was with a school group who could neither settle nor concentrate on an indoor activity. After about ten minutes of disruptions, I said, "Come on. Let's go for an exploration around the gardens."

In those days, the farmer had a herd of dairy cows and, as we walked along the path bordering the field they were in, I noticed the cow nearest the fence seemed to be very agitated.

Realising this was about to be a special moment, I said, while pointing to the animal which was now heaving, "Let's stop here and have a look at the cow nearest us."

The group stopped and, within a minute, the cow gave birth, her calf sliding out of her rear end then landing on the ground, covered in mucus. The new mother leaned down then gently licked it from head to tail. Now clean, the calf struggled to stand up on long, rickety legs and, once upright, instinctively searched for its mother's udder where it enjoyed its first suckle of milk. Throughout it all, the children had stood totally still, observing the proceedings without a word being said.

The teacher leaned across to me and whispered, "Sorry, it's time to go."

In silence the children walked back to the car park and climbed into their mini-bus. The teacher's assistant got into the driver's seat then, as the teacher opened the passenger door, she turned to me and said, "I don't suppose you could do that on every visit?" If only, I thought.

The Iver Nativity

In 2003, we held our second outdoor 'live' Nativity, this time with volunteers and staff playing all the characters. Geoff designed and built a cut-through stable and wooden manger. We had a small orchestra and even managed to borrow a real baby! Kareth, as narrator, microphone in hand, related the Nativity story which took place in and around the meadow, to the audience who were standing among the fruit trees.

While everybody sang 'Little Donkey', the story unfolded when Mary (Susi [Aris] Broad), riding on a real donkey, led by Joseph (Monique O'Toole Vige) were followed by Naomi (that year's National Grid graduate) who was camouflaged from head to toe in black, carrying a huge silver star at the end of a long pole. They made their way around the path outside the meadow, coming to a stop by the closed gate where they asked the innkeeper (Peter Hinson) if he had a room for them. After pointing to the stable in the meadow, he opened the gate, beckoning the young couple to come in. The donkey was taken off by a stable hand and Naomi, holding the star, slipped across the meadow and took up her place behind the stable.

Mary and Joseph then walked across to the stable and, once inside, shook out their cloaks and a blanket. While doing this, to distract the audience's attention from Mary and Joseph, the spotlight illuminated the star which twinkled and glittered in the darkness. Meanwhile, inside the stable, Mary was surreptitiously handed a real baby, not seen by the audience until she and Joseph had settled themselves on the hay bales which had been provided by the farmer next door. When the main spotlight then fell on the complete scene, I have to say, it looked incredibly realistic.

This scene was followed by me, handling the mini searchlight, swinging it round to highlight the Three Kings (Hazel, Henry and Roy, dressed in robes created by Poppy), being instructed by Herod (the narrator speaking his words), to go and find the new king. We all sang 'We Three Kings' while the spotlight illuminated their majesties as they walked slowly and regally across the bridge over the lake before heading to the meadow.

With the kings on their way, the main spotlight was then

turned to draw the audience's attention towards the top of the stone wall behind the vegetable plot. The Angel Gabriel (Gwen Hinson) – dressed in a white smock, with a huge pair of wings strapped to her back (courtesy of husband, Peter [the innkeeper]), slowly emerged above the top of 'The Garden of Time' side of the wall, with arms outstretched, and announced the birth of Jesus to the shepherds below. She was, in fact, balancing rather precariously on a ladder, with one leg being held by my husband, Ron and the other by my brother-in-law, David Axworthy! How Gwen balanced there while the audience sang 'While Shepherds Watched their Flocks' was nothing less than a miracle!

The spotlight then dropped to the base of the wall, to the next scene of three shepherds (Ron Simpson, Ian Pearce and his wife Mary), with a small flock of toy lambs, huddling together around a mock camp fire at the edge of the vegetable plot. At some point, they had somehow acquired a group of children who wanted to be shepherds as well, so tea towels had hastily been brought from the kitchen and draped around their heads, and gifts for the new baby wrapped in Christmas paper.

After receiving Angel Gabriel's message, in semi-darkness, Ian and Mary, both in their seventies, plus Ron S, picked up their lambs then, with the band of children trailing them, made their way in a crocodile to the fence enclosing the meadow. One by one, each climbed over the stile then walked to the stable where they stood around the crib.

The group by the stable was then joined, with perfect timing, by the Three Kings, who offered their gifts to the baby. Next, the children offered theirs and finally, the shepherds laid their sheep beside the, now sleeping, infant. While this scene played out, we all sang 'Away in a Manger'. We then brought the evening to an end with a rousing rendition of 'We wish you a Merry Christmas'.

A lovely comment, made by someone in the audience, was passed on to me: 'visually stunning'. Yes. It was worth all the effort.

Apple Day

Apple Day at Home Cottage Farm, Iver Heath, was another superb occasion in which we were caught up. Instigated in 1990 by the environment charity, Common Ground, it was an occasion to celebrate not only the incredible diversity of the apple but also to warn about the decline of both our orchards and the many apple varieties grown in this country. The official date for Apple Day is 21 October but events are held on the nearest weekend.

INSC joined forces with Peter and Pat Hinde, who owned the orchard at Home Cottage Farm, to celebrate Apple Day which, from its inception, proved very popular, with attendance rising every year, despite it raining at some point most years the Study Centre helped organise the event. We arranged for appropriate charity and trade stall holders to attend. Most of these were housed in the disused chicken sheds but, as the show expanded, they had their own 'village' on the grassy area.

The Iver volunteers undertook many of the activities throughout the years we were involved. The National Grid (NG) graduate and/or Mary Pomeroy sorted apple-related craft activities for the children. Nigel Phillips, who started out as a NG graduate but ended up running Horticultural Therapy (HT), undertook apple pressing and tasting. Jackie Naughton spent her day apple-face-painting. Vic and Jan Merril arranged for their local dog agility group to demonstrate and organised an apple-shaped jump for the event.

Throughout the day, the Iver catering crew – consisting of Elizabeth Whiting, Jill Myers, Lily Harris, Chris Hare and Hazel Hook– not only provided all the food but manned the catering marquee throughout the day. Clare organised and ran her teddy tombola stall, consisting of over a hundred toy bears. The bric-a-brac stall was run by Rosemary Thomas, Gwen Hinson and Teresa Cieciora. Teresa's husband, Witek, more often than not, came along to lend a hand wherever help was needed. Kareth offered alternative therapy taster sessions and, one year, led guided walks around the interesting little wood, telling her groups some folklore surrounding particular trees they could both see and touch. Poppy, then Monique, stood in a tiny shed on the corner of the 'open area', by the path which led to the main shop, giving talks about bees, bee products and how bee hives work. On several occasions, we had demonstrations of authentic besom broom making from Mick Walters of 'Micksticks' who had also carried out some traditional hedge-laying at the Study Centre. Out of harm's way, for a few years, we had an archery group of gentlemen which was popular.

Entertainment over the years included a ukulele band, who were a big hit and, on several occasions, the talented Vyners School pupils who played in the Vyners Swing Band, run by Perry Parsons. It was everyone's first experience of playing in an old chicken shed!

I, together with Henry Avery and Tony Myers, all armed with walkie-talkies, sorted out the car parking – both the entrance and exit to the show ground shared the same narrow lane!

We also had a line dancing team, consisting of Iver volunteers, giving their display. After our tenth anniversary dinner and dance, when the dancing was more formal, several volunteers suggested we could start line dancing lessons at the Centre so I arranged for my friends, Carole Southern and her husband John, who were regular line dancers, to put us through our paces. I say 'us' but my involvement was overseeing rather than taking part! Everyone enjoyed it and, when I realised they were rather good, I suggested they did a line dancing display at Apple Day but would have to think of a name for themselves. When nobody came up with anything appropriate, I christened them 'The Apple Tarts' which stuck! They were a great hit with the crowds.

The organisation, setting up and running of the day was exhausting but well worth all the effort. Despite some awful weather (it seemed to rain rather too frequently), it was a fun, very enjoyable and worthwhile venture, with many attendees saying how much they enjoyed it.

As well as running Apple Day at Home Cottage Farm, to coincide with this event, we launched 'Apple Fortnight' at the Study Centre, to celebrate the apple, as part of our educational programme. When a school group arrived, after the usual storing of lunch boxes then reading of the 'riot act', half the class would be driven in our mini bus to visit the orchard at Home Cottage Farm where they would see working bee hives, learn both how they are used by the bees and about the importance of pollination. This was followed by a visit to the big storage barn where the children were shown the large selection of named apple varieties which were grown on-site. Next, they had a guided walk around the farm to see other varieties of fruit being grown. These usually comprised of blackberries, raspberries, pears and plums. Finally, in one of the apple orchards, they were allowed to choose an apple to take home.

Back at the Centre, the remaining group would undertake a stick-and-paste activity on the life cycle of an apple. Next, they would take their turn in apple pressing, followed by tasting the juice. After the farm group returned, everyone let off steam on the assault course which was followed by hand washing then lunch, after which, roles were reversed.

After retiring from Iver, I was still involved in Apple Day and, in 2012, came up with the idea of creating a mini assault course for children which was given the thumbs up and proved to be really popular. Unfortunately, due to the confines of health and safety, plus insurance costs, we were not able to test the mettle of those under the age of eight, much to their disappointment.

The accolade that we had 'got it right' came towards the end of the afternoon. I realised there was a little boy, probably about three years old, charging round the course without a responsible adult in attendance. I asked the onlookers if he belonged to any of them. No, he didn't. After a few minutes, I noticed a rather anxious adult heading our way.

"Do you own a small boy in a red jumper?" I asked.

"Yes," came the reply.

"Don't worry," I said. "He's just about to start his third circuit. Great stamina."

I can still see his little face as it changed from pure joy to tragic disappointment when his father scooped him up.

In addition to our adult volunteers, we had four Royal Marine Cadets from Lima Group, Ruislip escorting the children around the course. These young people were invaluable, willingly offering assistance to those who needed a helping hand and always with a smile on their face. Oh, to be that age again and have their energy!

Looking back on what we achieved on our hand-made assault courses, built from bits of this, that and the other, over the years, we had given a lot of youngsters a lot of pleasure and the sheer joy of just being children at play.

Our Millennium Project

Our project was 'The Garden of Time' in which the old walled garden, – known originally as 'The Secret Garden', with its raised beds and bench beside the wall – would be transformed from a place few used, into three sections depicting the passing years. It would become somewhere visitors would be able to sit in a peaceful, aesthetically pleasing setting and pause to reflect on the past – and what the next millennium may hold.

This project was designed and constructed by Geoff. After entering via the old wooden door, visitors walked first past the Agricultural Revolution which portrayed rural life in England, with relics of a bygone age, e.g. rusting farm implements, an old enamel sink – now planted out – and a decaying farm building where plants had already taken root.

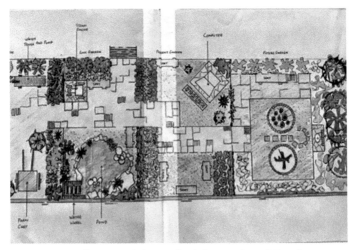

Geoff's original design for 'The Garden of Time'.
©Geoff Thomas

Next, through an open arch, were the gradual changes of the Victorian Industrial Revolution, with its invention of machines. Despite the boom in factory towns, the mill still had a place in the economy and this was depicted by a piston engine lying next to a small pond which had been dug out with the help of students from the local American School, into which trickled running water, provided by a waterwheel, made by Geoff, above the pond.

With the first computer having been invented at Bletchley Park during WWII, technology would be the future. Barry both designed and made two elegant copper structures, each of which represented a communications mast connecting computers on earth to satellites orbiting in outer space. He also created two copper people; one holding a bowl, the

The water wheel.
©Geoff Thomas

'The Garden of Time' and the communication masts.
©Geoff Thomas

other with arms outstretched to receive, depicting the future: man helping each other.

Actress Sheila Hancock OBE, as our guest of honour, kindly opened this project.

Our Millennium Calendar

During this special year, we also produced our own millennium calendar after I managed to persuade ten local companies, one day-care service group and, after some cajoling, my three sisters to join me[5]. Each sponsored one month of the calendar and each month was decorated with an illustration, produced by members of nine special needs groups plus three individual children.

The Reading Scheme

During the early years of school visits, when it was becoming more obvious some children had poor reading skills, I instigated a Saturday morning reading scheme, called 'Once upon a Time', for reluctant readers. To help, I had former teachers Brenda Ottaway and Jean Batchelor, plus another volunteer, Linda Sommerville, who all gave up their Saturday mornings for four years to help me run it. Jean not only helped with 'Once upon a Time' but also with mainstream school visits.

We used nature activities, such as making fat balls for the birds, to encourage the children to read which ingredients were needed and what to do with them. Worksheets proved

---

5   The sponsors can be found under the heading Companies, Firms and Groups which Supported Iver.

popular, as were gardening instructions, e.g. how to plant a bulb.

For one child, Brenda picked up the fact she needed an eye test because, if she was sitting to the side of the blackboard, in the days before white boards and computers, she could not see what was being written. Her parents were told and they had the problem sorted – reading glasses.

After many months of patient teaching and encouragement, when they had gained their confidence, each child both wrote and illustrated a natural-history-related story book, some of which had rather interesting titles, such as Charlie the Chicken, Freddy's Football Team and Ollie the Obstinate Worm.

Thanks to the generosity of the local printing company where Stan Bill, husband of Clare, worked, we were given beautifully printed copies of each book, free of charge.

One Christmas, the children on the scheme enacted a small Nativity. At the end of it, the father of the child reading the narration came up to me and said, "I just would not believe that's my daughter. She's so confident! Thank you" Apparently, she had been very shy and overshadowed by her two younger siblings.

Another father brought in his daughter's end-of-term report which stated 'a vast improvement in confidence and positive approach'.

One mother reported, for the first time, her son had read out a story he had written while at Iver, which was a first, as he had never before told her what he did, either at school or at the Centre.

SIX

VOLUNTEER KARETH PATERSON'S REMINISCENCES

HOW INSC CHANGED MY LIFE THROUGH COLLEGES, COLLAGES, COMPUTERS AND CAKES.

In 2020, when Sally asked me to write a short piece about my years at Iver and what the Centre meant to me, no matter how many times I used the cut-throat razor approach to remove all but the highlights, both my pen and memories refused to cooperate. Yes, I could have written a basic outline but in no way, shape or form would that have done justice to what I look back on as some of the happiest and most important years of my life. Fortunately, she allowed me to write this longer version.

'What Iver Nature Study Centre meant to me'. Eight

words which, in my case, could easily expand to many pages of accolades describing the uniqueness of the place and its 'Commander' (ref. '2001: A Space Experience') at the helm, not that she ever 'commanded' any of us to do anything she thought we could not achieve. Well, perhaps she did at times, such as, not long after becoming a regular volunteer, I was asked to create worksheets for five to eleven-year olds, for various 'Experiences', 'I'm Bored' holiday sessions and school visits. This would involve using my first-ever computer and an understanding of computer 'language', to be confident in using the more in-depth areas of the programs, plus getting to grips with internet researches, but I get ahead of myself.

I had frequently read articles about Iver Nature Study Centre in our local paper and one sunny, spring day in 1994 – on my drive home after a day's volunteering with the Bucks County Rangers in Black Park, while crossing the bridge spanning the M25, heading towards Uxbridge, having passed on numerous occasions, I decided to turn left at the end of the lane which was signposted to the Centre. As other volunteers have remarked, that sign was like a magnet, drawing many out of curiosity then capturing those who were to become the core volunteers.

Once in the gates, I was well and truly hooked. Over tea and a chat, I told Sally about my love of working with the natural environment. She then took me on a casual stroll around the gardens. A chance remark changed my life after I commented on the overgrowth smothering many plants in one particular area, known as 'The Countryside Game'. She asked if I could. I said I would. Looking back, she had cleverly and subtly reeled me in then landed me in her cache of volunteers, where I was to remain for the next twelve years.

One afternoon, while fighting the copious weeds or, as Sally called them, the right plants but just rather overgrown, she came over to see what I was doing and, after a 'normal' chat, dropped her bombshell. She was short of a leader for the school visit the following day and wanted me to take on the woodland activities with three groups, each consisting of about ten eight-year-olds. This was a subtle move on her part because, as a member of the volunteer rangers' team in the local Buckinghamshire country parks, the woodland was right up my street.

"But I'm not a teacher," I said. "I wouldn't know what to do."

Little did I realise then, Sally has the knack of knowing who the right person for the job is. The following afternoon, having emerged unscathed from a nail-biting birth by fire, I appreciated her method of teaching was the opposite to that of my childhood; sitting upright in an often chilly, draughty classroom, hands on the desk lid, listening to a teacher drone on about a subject which was of little or no interest to me. At Iver, teaching was always hands-on and fun. From then on, I was rarely on gardening duties at the Centre. However, having no experience of teaching, I decided to enrol for evening classes at Uxbridge College from where, two years later I emerged the proud recipient of a City & Guilds™ certificate.

My next challenge, asked in the subtle way Sally has, when one finds it impossible to say 'no!', was to produce a variety of worksheets, many including illustrations or diagrams. That led me back to college to study computing for semi-beginners, frequently with additional help from my friend, Jill Nicholas and Jenny, her ten-year-old daughter who knew more than both of us put together. Closer to hand, my neighbour, Ian Pearson, father of Jo and Ben, was my saviour when I was faced with my many brick walls. And yes, I left college with another certificate, plus a love for my computer.

During my twelve years as a volunteer, I also took on a variety of personae while teaching, both during the run of an 'Experience' and for schools' visits. In addition to these, for several years, to promote the Centre, I led, what I called, a 'Slow Motion', monthly stroll around the gardens, suitable for everyone young and old, whether able-bodied or not, during which we looked at plants, ponds, works in progress and, while strolling, I often told the group a little of the interesting history of the site, part of which goes back to Elizabethan times.

When our 'Experiences' were running, I became a rainforest inhabitant, an African djembe drummer, a Native American Indian, an astronaut and a Land Army girl. When we sang Christmas carols in the shopping centre in Uxbridge, I was one of the Three Kings. For 'The Science of Christmas', I created the INSC Christmas pudding recipe which the hundreds of visiting children thoroughly enjoyed making. In 2005, for 'Dig for Victory', I adapted my grandmother's WWII recipe for carrot buns for the children to make, then eat after lunch, or take home. Despite their lack of sugar, these proved to be extremely popular.

I helped year-round during school visits and, in the summer term, was feeder and keeper of 'pet' garden snails which I used when telling children, in a fun and interesting way, about why our woodlands are so important for nature, our own health and that of our entire planet.

Not long after starting at Iver, I qualified as a professional reflexologist then, over the years, as well as continuing to study other complementary therapies, also attended adult teaching courses, eventually becoming a professional therapy tutor for both Buckinghamshire and Middlesex Adult Education Centres. Sally was one of my practice 'bodies' for each new skill while I was learning and later, my demonstration 'body' when teaching. Although I now live in Scotland, when we meet, there is always time to reduce her stress levels using foot reflexology which is her favourite.

On one memorable occasion, the morning of the day we were due to open 'The African Experience', she was particularly under pressure. To calm her, I suggested a quick Indian head massage – her first. I had not long begun when she groaned while I massaged her taut scalp then gave a yelp at exactly the same moment two of the musicians, in traditional African costumes, popped their heads in the office door to ask something. They looked rather bemused to say the least, but we all had a laugh about it later.

An unforgettable highlight was in 2000, when Sally and I spent a week in Washington DC. Before our trip, she had arranged for us to visit the NASA school education department and, during our morning there, we were invited to take, without cost, whatever we thought would suit our mode of simple, hands-on teaching, suitable for five-to-eleven-year-old children. We wanted each child to have an idea, not so much about the technology of space travel and rockets, but about gravity and many of the things we now take for granted in our everyday lives, such as 'Velcro', bar codes, mobile phones with an integrated camera, CAT scans and scratch-resistance lenses for eye glasses. I have to say NASA was more than generous with their educational donations to our small Centre.

The following day, we had a fascinating exploration around the Smithsonian National Air and Space Museum where we touched a piece of rock brought back from the moon in 1969, saw the original spacesuits worn by the first two men to land on the Moon and were amazed at how flimsy Eagle, the Lunar Module LM-2 looked, covered as it was in what resembled copper-coloured baking foil. Both in Washington then over the course of our second week, when we stayed with my cousins in the San Francisco area, I realised Sally is incapable of passing a book shop!

Life at INSC was never boring. There was always another 'Experience' or project to be involved in, another request from Sally for 'I need a ...', 'could you create ...', 'what do you think about ...' No two days were the same, except for the sound of frequently heard laughter. I taught children, fund-raised, helped wherever it was needed, learned ballroom dancing and was one of 'The Apple Tarts' line dancing team for Apple Days at Home Cottage Farm.

We were constantly trying to find extra funding for the Centre and, toward that end, I indulged my loves of baking and complementary therapies. For two weekends every month, plus the bank holidays, for several years, I was one of two part-time managers at the Visitors' Centre, Denham Country Park, where there was a tiny cafe which offered hot and cold drinks, sweets and packaged biscuits but no fresh food. I filled a gap by offering home baking in return for a donation. Although some visitors put a token amount into the pot, the majority, many of whom had visited, or knew about, the Study Centre, were more than generous with their contributions.

Little by little, my donations pot grew fatter and went towards necessities such as a decent storage unit, a badge-making machine, complete with all accessories, a tunnel for 'the rabbit burrow run' on the assault course, specially designed white baseball hats for the *Iverana* crew, for '2001: A Space Experience' and also paid for other bits and bobs as and when needed.

On several occasions, some of my complementary therapy colleagues joined me in offering a variety of therapy taster sessions in return for donations which, after covering our own costs, we all passed on to the Centre. When both my local complementary therapy and reiki groups had to find larger premises for our monthly meetings, Iver was the perfect venue and, of course, our bookings brought the Centre much-needed income.

In 2006, my life at the Centre came to an end after being informed the rental for my little flat was about to increase dramatically. It was with great sadness I was forced, after forty years in England where I had enjoyed a variety of interesting careers and several years of volunteering, to return to Scotland, land of my childhood and of cheaper house prices, to begin the next chapter of my life.

I might be almost five-hundred miles away but am still in regular touch with Sally and several Iver volunteers. We really were, and still are, one large, happy family, and it is all thanks to one lady or, as one mother said to her child, when asked for the pot of glitter to decorate a collage, "the lie-die".

Thanks for the memories, Commander Sally.

SEVEN

THE NATIONAL GRID GRADUATE SCHEME HORTICULTURAL THERAPY ENBRIEF MAGAZINE

INTRODUCING SOME OF OUR GRADUATES AND HORTICULTURAL THERAPY PEOPLE.

'ENBRIEF' – NATIONAL GRID'S IN-HOUSE MAGAZINE.

A tremendous asset was the graduate scheme which National Grid instigated at their various centres throughout the country. For eleven months, a graduate was given remuneration while gaining experience of working with people of all ages, abilities and education, organising, devising activities and lots more. Over the years I was at Iver, we were blessed with some fantastic students. Poppy would often mother them and offer her home as accommodation if they did not have any place locally to stay whilst on the Scheme.

I must mention a few graduates who exceeded all expectations.

Susi [Aris] Broad proved to be extremely capable and was a delight to have around. She was followed by Georgina [King] Carlin, known as George, another very talented girl and great character. When Horticultural Therapy (HT) came to the Centre in July 1996, Susi returned to take on the job. After marrying, when she began her family, she and George job-shared and between them, ran it beautifully.

Together, they instigated the December 'Tree Dressing Day' activity at the Centre where HT groups dressed (decorated) trees in the theme of the day. They also held the inaugural flower show in the summer of 1998 which was so successful, it became an annual event. We sadly, had to say goodbye to both in March 2000 when Susi left to have her second baby and George took the opportunity to journey to New Zealand.

Beth [Grimwood] Reid, another delightful graduate who came to Iver on the NG Scheme, proved to be very efficient and hard working. One unusual memory I have of her, occurred during the run up to one Christmas when she appeared with a large and heavy netting sack containing Brussels sprouts, courtesy of her father who grew them commercially.

After her year with us, she went on to work for Groundwork Thames Valley, in the education sector. She married Barry Reid, one of our multi-talented volunteers who produced so much for the various 'Experiences'. One year, he designed and erected a superb outdoor scene of Father Christmas and his reindeers arriving in the sleigh, when we built an indoor winter grotto. He was also one of the creators of the 'Garden of Time' project.

Another fabulous person to have around was Cora [Cloughley] Hossain. Always willing, able, full of fun and constantly thinking up new ideas for 'I'm Bored' activities. She was also an enthusiastic astronaut during '2001: A Space Experience' when her specialist subject of teaching gravity proved very popular with our school groups. When her year came to an end, she went on to work for Groundwork Thames Valley, in the offices at Denham, before moving to study in Newcastle. She still keeps in touch, not only with me but also with many of the volunteers.

Father Christmas and his reindeer
©Sally Munn

Cora, Poppy and Kareth all put successful 'escape plans' in place, eventually moving away from the area but, a few years ago, the four of us enjoyed a short holiday in Derbyshire when we 'house sat' for the vicar who lived next door to Gwen Hinson's sister. As you can no doubt imagine, hours were spent laughing about all our experiences and 'Experiences', remembering those no longer with us but, most of all, enjoying being together for a few days.

When I began writing the story about my years at Iver, I asked Cora if she would like to write about what she got out of her year at the Centre. The following is her reply:

The National Grid Graduate Placement Scheme was a completely different 'package' compared to those my friends were applying to and it gave me the best work experience I have ever had. Nothing since has compared. The Scheme itself was great. There was a friendly national coordinator, and all the graduates met up several times at training and social events, but I was the lucky one; my placement was at Iver Nature Study Centre.

I will never forget the day I turned into the car park for the first time. After driving on motorways for six hours, I remember the verdant green all around, the wonderful log cabin, people busying about and laughter; lots of laughter. Just thinking about walking up the ramp to the cabin, or along the path by the pond, still gives me butterflies.

INSC was a place where everyone respected and valued everyone else:– the staff, the volunteers and all the individuals who visited. The small staff number was bolstered by the most incredible group of volunteers I have ever seen, or been part of, and this has to be down to the boundless enthusiasm, engagement and care of Sally, the Centre Manager – not to mention the crazy but unique ideas and the social gatherings!

With '2001: A Space Experience', which took place during my placement year, I will always remember the look of absolute amazement from the children after we had shown the launch of our space shuttle 'Iverana' video. They would look at us, then at the screen, then back to us – '…did you really go into space?' – wonderful.

I could pass through the Centre any one day and see people taking part in a craft activity in the main room, volunteers or others preparing for another visiting group in the next room, Poppy extracting honey from the comb/hives in the kitchen, volunteers tending to the different areas of the site, horticultural volunteers from a day-care centre busy in the potting shed, a school group investigating pond life and volunteers making a large sculpture of some sort for the next project …what a community!

There is so much more I could write, but the magic of Iver is difficult to put into words.

Monique O'Toole Vige, a delightful American lady, came as a volunteer then, after three months, was employed to run the HT programme. Throughout her tenure, she would keep us all in fits of laughter with her observations of life.

In May 2003, Syon Park was holding an exhibition called 'Countryside Live' for which we had created a mini orchard. As well as having an observatory bee hive and a display of apple varieties, we also offered activities which included rolling a beeswax candle, 'I Spy' in the orchard and apple crushing then tasting the juice. Because Monique had been unwell the day before the opening, I could not believe it when she turned up on the day.

"What on earth are you doing here?" I asked, incredulously.

Her reply was, "I didn't want to let you down."

In short, Monique was a very special person.

Nigel Phillips was introduced to Iver Nature Study Centre on the NG Scheme in 2004 and, during his time with me, was extremely supportive in everything we did. A very keen and respected horticultural therapist whose gentle nature meant he got on with everyone and they, in turn, admired and warmed to him. The following are his memories of INSC.

I was made redundant from a long career in the service sector and decided on a complete change. This took place at an environment charity in the Royal Parks where I volunteered and which subsequently led to INSC. At that time, Iver had extensive ponds, a meadow, a small wood, an impressive outdoor assault course, a maze and a walled garden. The grounds could be enjoyed throughout the year and each season had something to offer. I particularly liked the meadow which was a beautiful place in summer, with the abundance of wild flowers, bees and birds. It was a small area with two mowed paths leading to the centre and several apple trees dotted around. I enjoyed it in the early morning and later evening when there were few people around. I also remember the walled garden which led to the assault course. A Virginia creeper grew against the wall in that garden which was spectacular in autumn.

I pitched in and assisted Sally in the preparation and delivery of outdoor education programmes for children. Initially, it was quite daunting but I got used to it and befriended many wonderful volunteers who helped deliver these programmes and maintain the Centre. I have good memories of working there.

Not only children used the Centre as it was a community hub. People from all sectors of society visited and the educational programmes were adapted so marginalised and disabled people could enjoy the facilities. Gardening was introduced and I was involved with that. When the graduate programme expired, I continued working there as a horticultural therapist whilst studying for a 'Social and Therapeutic' qualification in horticulture. I qualified and have to thank Iver for giving me the confidence to go on and seek full-time employment as a horticultural therapist.

And, to finish, another HT person who did an excellent job devising activities for both able-bodied and those less able, using his superb artistic skills, was Stewart McLennan, known as Stu. He also used his talents to help with the production of a special birthday card from many of the users of the Centre to celebrate Her Majesty's eightieth birthday which, in due course, I delivered to Buckingham Palace in person.

'ENBRIEF'

National Grid produced an excellent in-house magazine called *ENBRIEF*, a newsletter for and about each of their environmental education centres. Their journalist was Sheila Barron, a lovely lady who was very supportive of Iver Nature Study Centre, as was Mark, the official photographer from National Grid. She once said to me, and I quote, 'we could produce a whole magazine just about what goes on at Iver!'

EIGHT
'I'M BORED' 1992-2008

A SELECTION OF THEMES AND A FEW STORIES FROM OUR SCHOOL SUMMER HOLIDAY WEEK FOR FIVE-TO-TEN-YEAR-OLD CHILDREN.

When they proved so popular, I decided to extend the half-day 'I'm Bored' sessions for five-to-ten-year-olds which we offered during the school holidays, into a week of summer holiday activities. Again, I called a meeting with my core volunteers and the National Grid graduate for that year, to talk through what might be feasible to occupy about twenty to thirty children over five consecutive days, Monday to Friday.

Once I established I had sufficient adults to head each of four groups, plus a few older children who could help out as necessary, the next stage was to come up with a main topic for that week, with relevant daily activities which would be educational, yet fun. Over the years, we offered a wide variety of topics and, in the years we had a special 'Experience', the activity that summer would relate to it. Even if any child had visited with their school, the summer activities were geared towards fun rather than school learning and, instead of working in twos or threes, they would often work as a team, assisted by an adult and at least one helper.

We adapted what we used for school visits, making everything fun. 1992, the first year, was very much the learning curve when we found our feet. With each successive year, we came up with different ideas plus occasional local outings, and knew we were on to a winner when many of the children turned up year after year. Several, when they were too old to take part, came along as helpers.

The summer week was run along the same lines as school visits, i.e. 'the riot act', putting lunch bags into the big bin, the assault course, proper hand washing etc. The biggest difference was, having five days to fill, there had to be lots of excitement, hands-on arts and crafts, with everything suitable for a wide age range although, when necessary, adapted for the youngest group which occasionally had a child less than five years of age. We could not repeat things from previous years as the same children came time and time again and finally, there had to be a theme for the week. At the start of the first day, each child was given a large paper folder. Everything they made during the week was kept in this. It also contained a sharpened pencil and a specially designed INSC diary in which, before leaving for home, they wrote about what they had done that day.

The following are some of the summer 'I'm Bored' themes and a few stories.

1992: A Different Activity Every Day

This first year was my learning curve, and I was determined to have every child enjoy their week of environmental activities. Over the five days, the children made finger puppets, worked with clay and wood, pressed flowers, enjoyed a nature trail rally and, on 'The Countryside Game'[6] area, competed against each other to be first to the finishing line. They also cross-stitched animal patterns and made textile creations with Sheila Gray who, in 1998, when we ran 'The African Experience', gave several displays of belly dancing. The highlight of the week was learning about bats and the children were thrilled to see the real thing when a professional bat-handler visited.

1997: Circus Skills

Over the course of five days, the children had fun stilt walking, making 'balancing' butterflies, creating then painting salt dough clowns, trying to balance on various objects such as an up-turned flower pot, stilts, an empty tin, a brick on its side etc. After lunch one afternoon, we had a face-painting session when each child painted a partner's face with a circus theme, – clowns being the most popular design. For both teamwork and coordination, they laid out the life-sized blue whale jigsaw in the main car park.

---

6   'The Countryside Game' was played like Ludo but with questions about the environment. For details, see chapter one 'In the Beginning'.

One activity they all loved was to show how important eye to hand coordination is. This game, sometimes known as 'Splat the Rat', was done as a team activity, with one person dropping the rat (a bean bag) into a metre-long plastic tube at a forty-five-degree downwards angle. The person at the lower end had to splat (hit) the rat with a soft club when it shot out the end of the tube, otherwise it fell on the floor. It was not as easy as it looked but great fun was had by everyone.

1998: Pirates

Very hands-on and colourful. Each child made their own costume from our boxes of materials, bits of paper, leaves, twigs and whatever else they could lay their hands on and, of course glitter, glue, lots of poster paint, beads and knick-knacks. All these combined to make hats, bandanas, swords, eye patches, jewellery and a map for an opposing team to use for a treasure hunt. They listened to extracts of classical music, including 'The Swan' (Saint-Saëns), 'Mars' (Elgar) and 'Morning' (Grieg), then created interpretive dances or movements. Ted Sellars, a member of the Uxbridge RAF band, whose daughter was one of the children that year, played the flute for 'The Sailors' Horn Pipe'.

1999: The Natural World

We began by visiting nearby Rowley Farm, Wexham, then in the process of applying for organic status, where the children learned the differences between organic farming and mass-produced food. Back at INSC, after finishing their packed lunch, they had the opportunity of trying a variety of organic, natural foods, including carrot sticks, cucumber, grapes and strawberries. There were also cherries, and one bright spark organised a cherry-spitting competition to see who could eat their cherry then spit the stone furthest from the patio towards the meadow. This proved extremely popular and went on until there were no cherries left. If memory serves me correctly, one of the younger boys became champion.

2000: Adventures in Wonderland

Loosely based on the Lewis Carroll story, Kareth adapted Alice's adventures by writing a story containing clues as to what that day's activities would be, which she read, one short chapter per morning, before the fun and games began. These included: being giants looking at the tiny pond-life found in each of our three ponds, playing croquet around the maze, using hedgehogs and flamingos (handmade, not real ones!), making flowerpot frogs, solving riddles and making dozens of jam tarts and little cakes. On the final day, each child wore something they had made or brought with them on the day, relating to a character from the book and, for the final hour, we all sat in the garden to enjoy a mad hatter's tea party in warm sunshine.

'2001: A Space Experience'

Our most ambitious week with lots of glue, paint, explosions and mess the entire week and all great fun. Each of the four groups took the name of a planet: Venus, Neptune, Mars or Jupiter.

Activities included making a rolled-paper rocket, complete with fins, then inserting a straw through the base.

After taking a very deep breath, each child launched their rocket from its straw. The next activity was much more exciting – making real rocket fuel to show how the energy of expanding gasses forces a rocket skyward!

Using a plastic lemonade bottle, after pouring vinegar on to bicarbonate of soda, quickly corking the top then standing well back, the group waited for the explosive launch. Needless to say, they were amazed and excited when the fizzing, expanding, liquid forced the rocket upward then across the meadow at great speed.

Another popular activity was creating the solar system inside a shoe box, painted pale blue outside and darker blue inside. This was fun, messy, involved lots of glitter and glue but was most impressive when finished. Each box was filled with cut-out and decorated rockets, asteroids, stars and planets, some stuck to the sides, many suspended on black thread from the top of the box.

Learning the acronym 'My Very Elegant Mother Just Sat Upon Nine Porcupines', using the first letter of each word to remember the names of the nine planets, in order from the sun, was popular. These were: Mercury, Venus, Earth, Mars, Jupiter, Saturn, Uranus, Neptune and Pluto.[7]

Kareth, again using her computing skills, created a unique end-of-week 'newspaper', called the *Iverana Informer*, which comprised six pages of comments, all taken from the children's daily diary entries, using their words and spellings. A copy of the *Informer* was put in each child's folder as a souvenir of their week.

---

7   In 2001, 'P' for Pluto was still one of the nine.

WHAT AN EXPERIENCE!

WE WENT TO THE SPACE SHIP. (IT'S IN A TENT). Rachel (Mars)	We had lots of fun From Jordan (Mars)	**THE SUN** The sun is the biggest star. It is very hot. 6,000°C. A hot day on Earth is 30°C from Harriet (Neptune)
Zoe (Pluto group) wrote: We first made pop cards then we painted our boxes, then we went on the ass *Editor's note: We are left to assume she then went on the assault course but, at Iver, you never know.*	**We lernt about space ships then we did the fit thing and put our hands in gung.** **We made pupits.** **We went on the op salocause.** **We had lunch, it started to rain but we had a dry place.** From Connor (Neptune)	Today we played an amazing game but it wasn't amazing. Lastly we did paint a box. There are 9 planets in the Solar System. Another one been's seen. From Kim (Pluto)
The Space Experience It all started on a monstroes Monday at Iver nature study. We were just meeting our group leaders when we saw something A mazing. A rocket had landed right infront of us. The door opened and we suddenly encourmted an alien named Fred. He was the coulor of bogey green. He began speaking in alien launguege but we couldn't understand him. He started following a smell that was really the Venus fly trap. He touched the shoebox it was in and he shrunk. Suddenly he wobbled and fell into the Venus fly trap. It snapped shut and crushed him to crumbs so we thought we were safe at last. By **Eilish and Megan.**	**JOKE** **Knock knock,** **Whos there,** **Lettuce,** **Lettuce who,** **Let us in** **and you'll find out!** By Gemma Crickmore (Neptune) --- **SPACE ROCKETS** At Iver Nature Study Centre we were talking about Space rockets. We made some Space Rockets and looked at the stars, sun, moon and planets. We have learnt about most of the planets, Mars, Jupiter, Venus and Uranus. From Catherine Underhill (Neptune)	From Venus group, Florence wrote: Today I had my photo taken again for a local paper. (I'm famous!) Christopher in Venus Group wrote a very interesting entry in his Mission Log Book - Forst we di d a hopscoc game. Ten we mad pupits.

A page from the *Iverana Informer*

©Kareth Paterson

2002: Italy

A hands-on week which included making and throwing pizza dough, some of which, inevitably, landed on the floor, but we had plenty spare, plus a few emergency packs of bought pizza base. I led this activity, astonishing the children, and myself, with my dough-throwing expertise. Each child created their own little pizza which Geoff cooked in the pizza oven in 'The Olive Grove', where we all ate lunch together for the first time ever. Normally, each group chose an area of the gardens where they wanted to have lunch.

On the final day, I recall Kareth's group, the five-to-seven-year-olds, singing a song she taught them, in Italian, with actions, to the tune of 'Frère Jacques', which impressed everyone, including the parents who made up the audience.

Buongiorno! Buongiorno!   (Good morning!)
Come stai? Come stai?   (How are you?)
Molto bene grazie. Molto bene grazie,
                                         (Very well thank you,)
Arrivederci! Arrivederci!   (Bye-bye!)

At the start of the following year's 'I'm Bored', two of the boys astonished me by singing a perfect rendition!

2003: Bees

With bees being the theme for the week, we tried to cover all the interesting facts about these gentle, very necessary insects, without which life, as we know it, would cease to be. With Poppy's help, the children learned to spin honey, tasting the result afterwards and, on one day, made biscuits and little cakes containing honey. A local lady helped each child make a stained-glass bee. Kareth wrote a rhythmic marching chant which was used when moving between activities and en route to the assault course. It went like this, with repeat after repeat until we reached our destination:

Everywhere we go-o,
People always ask us
Who we are.
So then we tell them we are all
Buzzy bees from INSC
And, if they can't hear us
We buzz a little louder!

2004: Natural History and Films

After watching a few scenes from a different film on each of the five mornings: *A Bug's Life, The Jungle Book, Finding Nemo, Brother Bear* and *The Lion King*, that day's theme was used for natural history fun learning.

The wide variety of activities included exploring bugs and beasties, clay modelling, painting then tie-dyeing fabric and making musical instruments, followed by playing African rhythms on these and on Kareth's collection of djembe drums and percussion instruments. There was also pond dipping, water and rainforest fun, plus tasting varieties of tropical fruit. Thanks to volunteers Vic and Jan, the children were introduced to small and large snakes and, for the enthusiasts, were allowed to handle some. Making Native American leather jewellery and dream catchers was also a hit. As ever, baking, again based on honey, followed by eating the results, was very popular.

The natural history mural
©Sally Munn

Each afternoon, to create a backdrop for the annual end-of-week concert, the children added handmade and painted details around the theme of that week until, by Friday, they had produced a huge environmental mural which the helpers and I attached to one wall of the marquee. In front of this, the children sang and acted the song, 'The Bare Necessities', from The Jungle Book, to their audience, comprising mainly of their relatives.

2005: WWII 'Dig for Victory' and the Home Front

That year, there were forty children for the week! Activities included first aid, make do and mend, rag rug making, planting vegetable seeds, rationing and baking carrot buns. They listened, in complete silence, to Ted, an ex-navy survivor from WWII, telling them his story of being torpedoed at sea and how he survived.

Every child painted a blank ceramic tea plate with either a Spitfire or a carrot and potato template motif. Jenny Pearson, Jo and Ben's mother, also helped from home, painting motifs on the spare plates. The following day all the plates were given to a local lady for firing in her kiln before being returned to each child as a memento of INSC and the Home Front.

On the final day, everybody made WWII food-ration sandwiches for lunch from a variety of fillings available in the 1940s. Spam and corned beef proved the most popular and Marmite, the least. Next, they ate their way through their home baking, including carrot buns, made using Kareth's WWII recipe. Lunch ended with jelly and ice cream which was a big hit all round, although there were complaints from some older boys who said their portion was too small, until I reminded them there was a war on and food was rationed. They accepted this, although several still queued in the hope there might be second helpings.

During this year in particular, it was noticeable how inept many children were when using implements such as cutlery, scissors, needles for sewing and craft work in general.

2006: Adventures around the World

Kareth wrote another story, this time about two children going around the world in five days and their adventures on each continent. Before starting, everyone sat on the floor listening for clues as to what activities they would be doing during that day. These included:

South America: creating a piñata, pouring sweets into its body then smashing their handiwork to get at the goodies inside. They also made, baked then ate chocolate biscuits, having learned the cocoa bean was first found in South America.

North America: constructing Native American headdresses from material, paper, feathers and beads.

Europe: pizza making – again, I demonstrated my prowess at throwing the pizza dough! Voted top activity was eating Italian vanilla ice cream! No surprise there.

Africa: making, then playing, musical instruments.

China: using chop sticks to pick up rice, carrot sticks and noodles.

India: dressing up in traditional costumes supplied by two mothers, who also taught the children a traditional dance.

Japan: writing Japanese letters using pen and ink; a first for everyone.

The final day finished in New Zealand and, for their display to parents and friends, the children had learned with, rugby fan/young volunteer, Ben Pearson's help, to sing in the Maori language while performing the haka, with actions. As you may know, the New Zealand Maori haka ends with the dancers making rude facial gestures at the enemy or the opposition, in this case, their parents! Needless to say, every participant made the most of frowning, glaring and sticking out their tongue while rolling their eyes at the guests!

2007: A Week of All Sorts

With many of my core team of 'I'm Bored' volunteers having retired, moved away, or being unavailable, Kareth drove south from Scotland to help for the week. There was no theme as such, although we still focussed on the natural world. For a change, we had a mixed bag of activities which included a walk around Mansfield Farm, next door to us, where the children met horses, sheep, cows and chickens. Halfway round, one little innocent at the back of the crocodile drew everyone's attention to the chickens playing 'King of the Castle'. The problem was, the King of the Castle, in this case, was the cockerel doing what cockerels do!

Using the mini bus, we visited Home Cottage Farm, where Apple Day was held annually in October. Here, we picked raspberries and plums which we made into jam to go with scones, oatcakes and biscuits, all made by the children. On the last day, after performing their country dance in front of their parents and a group of invited senior citizens, the children served afternoon tea, consisting of their homemade jams and baking, to all our guests.

That should have been the end of that week's activities but I got the surprise of my life when the children then sang a song they had been practising in secret, having changed the words of 'Happy Birthday' to 'thank you, thank you, dear Sally' etc. Lovely.

2008: The Environment and a Touch of Personal Hygiene

Again, Kareth made the long journey down from Scotland to help us for the week of diverse activities. We had fewer children than previously and it was noticeable how, over the course of three or four years, the majority were now unable to use scissors, sharpen their pencil or work independently. Their attention span was also shorter than in the past.

As well as doing fun-based environmental sessions of pond, wood, meadow, bees and the rainforest, for a complete change, we put in a day of personal hygiene, with practical sessions on hand washing and teeth cleaning, mainly to show

how much water is wasted when the tap is left to run. To demonstrate the latter, each child brushed their teeth for the recommended two minutes (timed), rinsing from a mug of water then spitting into a bucket. As soon as they began brushing, one of the helpers opened the tap of the tea urn which was filled with cold water and left the water trickling into a clean bucket for the two minutes. All the helpers and children were amazed, not only for the length of time they should spend brushing their teeth but at how much water was wasted by leaving the tap running. Each child was allowed to keep their toothbrush, as a reminder of how to brush their teeth properly.

There was a funny story at the start of this particular week. After I had given the children an outline of what they would be doing during the week, I finished by telling them I would teach them a special country dance which they would perform in front of their parents on the final day. An eleven-year-old boy helper put his hand up and asked, "Please, miss. Do we helpers have to do the lap dancing as well?" I was, and still am, lost for words!

*

On the final day of every 'I'm Bored' week, I awarded each helper with a 'Certificate of Thanks' and also presented two further certificates; one to 'The Child of Character', the other to 'The Pain of the Week'. The winner of the latter, inevitably one of the boys, always accepted it with a grin two feet wide.

There was also what was to become a ritual for the last

day, the initial one having been instigated in the early days by the 'big boys' after discovering the hose, used to water the plants and clean the vehicles, had been left attached to the tap. On the first occasion, the boys had it all worked out; wait for me to leave the marquee, then attack, which they did, extremely successfully!

I was soaked from head to toe, surrounded by a couple of dozen children and several parents, all laughing their heads off. Needless to say, when I chased the culprits, they dropped the hose and ran for it!

'Sally's annual soaking', as it was known thereafter, became a ritual and, following that first surprise attack, I kept a spare set of clothes in the office for the last day of the 'I'm Bored' week.

Sally's annual soaking
©Kareth Paterson

One special memory I have from these years is a mother telling me, on the first day she brought her daughter, she was very reluctant about attending. By the Friday, she could hardly wait to get to the Centre!

NINE

2009
MY FAREWELL

A PERSONAL TRIBUTE TO EACH AND EVERY INSC VOLUNTEER.

When retirement loomed, before handing over the keys to a new manager, I arranged a final Christmas dinner evening for my volunteers, during which I could celebrate the achievements we had accomplished together over the years. I wanted to make the evening special but also wanted to pay a final tribute to all my volunteers, both past and present. The following is an adaptation of that night's speech which, I hope, says it all.

Over the years, there have been many books, poems, plays and films, with love being the glue which binds each. When

I felt the urge to write my story about Iver Nature Study Centre and the love shown by my volunteers which made it the success it became, those first thoughts were of where and how to begin. Where indeed? Iver meant a lot to me and I had dedicated eighteen years to running a two-acre wildlife garden, stuck between the M25 which was, and still is, pumping out carbon monoxide at an alarming rate on one side and the National Grid substation on the other.

I honestly believe what we created at the Centre was unique and the result of sheer hard work, given freely by all my volunteers and supporters of INSC. Our success came down to three 'C's: Care, Commitment and Compassion.

I, personally, loved Iver when it was all-singing, all-dancing, with people coming and going all the time – although, of course, such distractions were not conducive to getting any office work done. I loved hearing laughter, seeing the care everyone put into whatever faced them, and I watched friendships form. When I needed help, it was always freely given, and I was humbled at the professionalism each person put into whatever task was asked of them. I marvelled at the catering team producing mounds of food for launches, 'Experiences', Open Days, Apple Days or any other events held at the Centre. Often these hardy souls had to stand for hours, serving, replenishing or clearing up afterwards, but there was never one word of complaint from any of my 'Iverites'.

The education team was something else. They dealt with nightmare children and, even worse, appalling adults, yet they still turned up when I phoned asking for help and support. Often, when faced with teaching a subject of which they had no experience, they would head to the library or, in later years, the internet, to learn enough to feel confident about that particular topic. Unless we were au fait with the subject, which one of us could have imagined feeling comfortable when explaining gravity, the many uses of the plains buffalo or how important the rainforests and bees are to humanity?

The gardening team worked wonders in the jungle which passed for a two-acre wildlife garden – it certainly lived up to the term 'wildlife'. Even after all the years I worked at Iver, the garden was never as I had hoped but I think we all enjoyed its informality, nooks and crannies and perhaps that in itself was what made the Centre what it was.

Looking back at all the 'Experiences' we put on, I am still amazed at their success. As I said in my final speech, despite the sheer hard work of getting everything ready for the launch, then the school and group visits, we had fun, mixed in with chaos, achieving the best 'Experiences' we could, considering the tiny budget allowed for such events. For me, there was a warm glow of satisfaction, knowing a job had been done to the best of everyone's ability and which would benefit others. Recalling the many 'thank-you' letters I received from those who took part in the 'Experiences', assured me we achieved what we had set out to do.

The Centre was there to provide a service to the community and I strove to do just that. We had standards, and every single volunteer took responsibility seriously. I know I was called old-fashioned at times but, if that meant we educated our visitors, stimulated their brain, used each of their five senses, gave children sharp pencils, clipboards, scissors and paint and had them help with washing-up on many occasions – and we spoke the Queen's English, as opposed to jargon – what is the problem?

Whilst managing Iver, I must have run every gamut of emotion known to mankind.

Dogmatic. That's me. I refused to change my basic principles then, and the same stands today.

Sadness. I often think of the volunteers no longer with us due to retirement or moving away from the area and those who have died.

Adamant about getting things right in all we did at the Centre.

Hysterical with laughter, still to me, one of the most wonderful sounds in the world, over some of the antics my key volunteers got up to.

Apologetic for all the times I drove my volunteers witless with my opinions and demands. I still recall occasions when I asked the impossible and they, bless them, came up with answers and possible solutions.

Gratitude to all my volunteers for coming into my life, enriching it beyond measure.

Pride in all we achieved through the years. By circumnavigating the walls of indifference and using our professionalism, generosity of spirit, creativity and originality, we attained all our goals. I am still astounded at what we, as a team, achieved out of almost nothing, and it was all down to my volunteers, without whom Iver Nature Study Centre would not have become the success it was.

Now, twelve years later, looking back to my eighteen years as the Centre Manager, I remember being constantly physically and mentally exhausted but, despite this, they truly were years filled with laughter, happiness, enjoyment, accomplishments and the most wonderful friendships. I could not have written my Iver story had it not been for my band of loyal volunteers who shared my journey around every bend, up and down every hill, to outer space and back. This is my tribute to all of them for being a part of Iver Nature Study Centre and an important part of my life. I would not have missed any of it for the world.

Every volunteer attending this final dinner received a copy of Peter's sketch.

Peter's sketch of the pond at Iver Nature Study Centre.
©Peter Hinson

TEN

HIGHLIGHTS OVER THE YEARS
1990–2007

MEMORABLE MOMENTS AND OCCASIONS.

1990

21 September   Sir John and Lady Mills opened Iver Nature
                Study Centre.

1991

June   INSC volunteer Keith Macqueen won a Barclays
                Innervision Certificate of Merit.

November   Debbie Greenwood visited INSC to collect the
                Penny Appeal donations for BBC's *Children in
                Need*.

December   The first outdoor Nativity and candlelight carol concert took place at the Centre.

1992

May   Sally Magnusson opened 'The Countryside Game'.

October   Pupils from both Iver Heath County First School and Meadow School won a bronze award at the Royal Anniversary Trust Awards for the creation of 'The Countryside Game' and for building a rockery, respectively.

November   INSC volunteer Anne Smith won the Gulbenkian Award for Environmental Endeavour.

1993

January   INSC won a Commendation in the Colonel Sanders Environmental Awards.

May   Penelope Keith OBE opened the redevelopment of the patio area.

An outdoor tea dance took place at the Centre.

October   David Bellamy, between local appointments, stopped by for lunch at INSC.

December   The first 'Tree Dressing Day' took place which was won by one of the groups from the Slough Education Unit (SEU).

The INSC volunteers went carol singing in The Pavilions shopping centre, Uxbridge.

1994

January   'The Rainforest Experience' was opened by Rocky, a blue and white macaw.

Lord Arran, Environment Minister, visited INSC.

February   Baloo and King Louis, of The Jungle Book film fame, visited 'The Rainforest Experience'.

March   INSC volunteer, Graham Myers, won Barclays Innervision Regional Certificate of Merit.

April   National Grid gave more land to INSC to create the 'Get down to Nature' mini assault course, showing how animals move.

May   INSC received a commendation in the 1993 Royal Institution of Chartered Surveyors' Awards.

July   Hillingdon Parkinson's Disease Society donated £50 to INSC to purchase an extra-long hose reel.

November   The Kew Education Outreach trailer visited INSC for a week.

National Grid sponsored 'The Four Seasons' internet computer program.

December   1st Richings Park Girl Guides donated a mini-fridge to the Centre.

1995

January   Tracy Edwards MBE, the first round-the-world yachtswoman, launched 'The Sea Experience'.

February   The Cherries, Flackwell Heath, created a wall mosaic in 'The Secret Garden'.

April   Launch of the 'Dig for Victory' exhibition, commemorating the fiftieth anniversary of the end of WWII in Europe.

September   Martyn Lewis CBE, BBC news presenter, visited INSC to see the Centre's newly installed National Grid's 'The Four Seasons' internet program in action.

Sir John and Lady Mills made a return visit to INSC to celebrate the Centre's fifth birthday.

National Grid held its Electricity in the Community forum at INSC.

December   Lloyd's Bank, Uxbridge donated money towards the Centre's canopy over the patio.

1996

February   INSC volunteer Kareth Paterson was presented with the British Airways Award for Excellence in the Community.

March   'The Tuesday Volunteers' completed the raised pond at INSC, made possible with sponsorship from BT Countryside for All.

May   Mohawk, Chris Brant and the Clan National Dancers opened 'The Culture and Customs of Native American Plains and Woodland Indians' project, for which INSC volunteer Sue Taylor constructed a life-sized buffalo.

August   The Centre held its first 'Iver Awards' ceremony at the annual volunteers' lunch, at which Bill Harris won Volunteer of the Year.

October   INSC became one of the main organisers of Apple Day at Home Cottage Farm, Iver Heath; a family fun day celebrating the versatile apple.

November   Work began on the log cabin extension to provide a much-needed large activity room, plus two small offices.

December   INSC volunteers and staff created a Nativity tableau, with real baby, for our carol singing fund raising event in The Pavilions shopping centre, Uxbridge.

1997

February
'The Rainforest Experience', sponsored by BAA Heathrow and the Committee on the Public Understanding of Science (COPUS), was opened by Jackie Zammit of Rainforest Road Show. Over its eleven-week run, it attracted over two thousand visitors.

May
Bob Holness launched the Parkinson's Education Pack for schools, sponsored by BT Countryside for All and Hasbro.

July
The second National Grid Community Forum took place at INSC to show their shareholders how some of their investment was used to support community events, such as those held at the Centre.

September
The 'Once upon a Time' reading scheme, held on Saturday mornings and sponsored by Glaxo Wellcome, was launched. The demand to help reluctant children read necessitated two groups being formed.

1st Wexham Scouts renovated a garden bench which they donated to INSC for 'The Secret Garden'.

Re-launch of both the Centre's expansion and the sensory garden.

October   1st Wexham Scouts both designed and built the 'hedgehog hop' in the 'Get down to Nature' assault course.

National Grid sponsored INSC's stand at the Slough Focus on Business exhibition. Our presentation showed examples of how National Grid supports the environment through its various Centres. Our layout, designed by INSC volunteer, Peter Hinson, won the Award for Best Stand.

INSC created a mini-orchard in the meadow and hosted an Apple Fun Day. J. Sainsbury plc donated one thousand apples which we then sold in aid of both the Hillingdon Branch of the Parkinson's Disease Society and the Hayes Stroke Club.

December   Volunteers and staff of the Centre produced a Nativity scene, again with a real baby, at the annual carol singing fund raising event at The Pavilions shopping centre, Uxbridge.

1998

January   INSC held a 'Getting to know you' gathering where John Randall, MP for Uxbridge, introduced the Study Centre to local businesses, to seek their support for future projects.

February   Initial plans were drawn up and Wimtec Environmental, Iver Heath, part-sponsored research ideas for the Centre's millennium project; 'The Garden of Time'.

Hasbro Ltd, Stockley Park, donated money towards the 'Once upon a Time' Saturday morning reading scheme.

March   'The African Experience', sponsored by BAA Heathrow, featuring an Egyptian pyramid and tomb, the Sahara desert and the savannah grasslands opened, then ran for ten weeks, attracting over eighteen hundred visitors.

April   INSC organised a Parkinson's Awareness Day and, with proceeds from a raffle, donated £680 to the Hillingdon Branch of the Parkinson's Disease Society.

May   Tyler Rounding, an American student, organised the renovation of 'The Countryside Game' as part of his Eagle Scout Award.

June   INSC launched its own coverage of World Cup 98 by transforming the pyramid from 'The African Experience' into a giant scoreboard and using the event to promote literacy, numeracy, geography and healthy eating.

World Oceans Day was celebrated with a fortnight of activities to learn about oceans, seas and seashores.

A thirteen-seater minibus was presented to the Study Centre by Judith Chalmers OBE, President of The Lady Taverners, on behalf of The Lord's Taverners.

July   6th Eastcote Beavers donated £50 worth of books to Iver's 'Once upon a Time' reading scheme.

Susi Aris and George King, of the Horticultural Therapy section, staged the first INSC flower show which was a tremendous success.

October   INSC again helped to organise Apple Day at Home Cottage Farm, Iver Heath.

The Study Centre took part in 'The World's Biggest Coffee Morning' fundraising event.

December   A Christmas Grotto was created in the Study Centre.

INSC again played host to the National Grid shareholders, showing them first-hand how some of their investment supported community events.

1999

April   INSC held An Evening with Seckow Keita, a Senegalese musician who later went on to find fame in the world of music.

INSC volunteer Kareth Paterson began her monthly 'Slow Motion' guided walks around the Centre. Members of the public were taken on a tour of the grounds to learn about the history of the site and what activities were taking place at the time.

July   Launch of 'The Rainforest Experience', now a permanent project, situated in an outdoor poly tunnel, was sponsored by BAA Heathrow.

INSC took a stall at the Royal Windsor Horse Show.

September A donation from Lincoln Financial Services, Uxbridge was used to build the bee hut; a place where volunteer Poppy Thomas could store the bee paraphernalia.

2000

March   Mike McTyre, from the American Scout Group 402, Uxbridge, as part of his Eagle Scout Award, organised construction of 'The Caterpillar Crawl' in the 'Get down to Nature' mini assault course.

May   The extension to the Horticultural Therapy area was opened, thanks to the generosity of Lincoln Financial Services, Uxbridge.

July   Iver's millennium project, 'The Garden of Time', landscaped by the Centre's part-time gardener, Geoff Thomas, was opened by Sheila Hancock OBE.

September   INSC celebrated its tenth anniversary with a dinner and dance at The Bull Hotel, Gerrards Cross.

October   Apple Day at Home Cottage Farm was, once again, a great success, despite the almost constant rain.

December   With over twenty staff, clients and volunteers, plus the addition of a keyboard player and a violinist, the INSC annual carol singing fund raiser in The Pavilions shopping centre, Uxbridge, was a great success.

2001

April   '2001: A Space Experience' finally lifted-off after the initial launch was aborted, due to the countrywide outbreak of foot-and-mouth disease. A series of events, under the banner 'Spaced Out', took place between June and September. One included a visit by NASA astronaut, Dr Don Lind, accompanied by his wife.

June — BT Cellnet became the first company to be involved with INSC and Corporate Social Responsibility (CSR) when employees from both Slough and Leeds held a team-building day at the Study Centre.

August — A special launch day was organised to acknowledge BAA Heathrow, Lincoln Financial Services, Martin-Baker Aircraft, National Grid and Groundwork Thames Valley, all of whom sponsored '2001: A Space Experience'.

The Study Centre held its eleventh anniversary lunch and fifth 'Iver Awards' ceremony.

September — The final day of '2001: A Space Experience' was celebrated by holding an open day. During the project's five month run, an estimated four thousand plus people visited.

October — The Study Centre again organised Apple Day at Home Cottage Farm, Iver Heath which was very successful, with over seven hundred people attending. The Apple Tarts, a newly formed line dancing team, made up of INSC volunteers, gave their first performance to an appreciative audience.

2002

March   Iver launched 'Growing with Gardening'; a children's Saturday morning gardening club which proved popular and ran for two years.

May   To mark the Queen's Golden Jubilee, INSC held a family fun day.

July   Lady Lucinda Lambton opened 'The Olive Grove', a landscaped patio, designed by our part-time gardener, Geoff Thomas, with its centrepiece consisting of an authentic, hand-built brick pizza oven. This project was made possible, thanks to financial help from Sacla Ltd who also donated a generous supply of pesto sauce for our unique INSC pizzas.

October   INSC helped organise the annual Apple Day at Home Cottage Farm, this year sponsored by South Bucks District Council and BAA Heathrow.

November   A 'Tree Dressing Day' was held at the Centre.

2003

March   INSC volunteer Chris Hale began her monthly informal and relaxed watercolour classes.

April   An American Scout group from Surrey spent a day working hard in the gardens.

May   The Centre took part in National Moth Night.

The INSC Open Day was transferred from September to May Day for two reasons: better weather and to give us more time to organise Apple Day in October.

At the 'Countryside Live' event at Syon Park, Brentford, INSC created an orchard, with an apple display plus an observatory beehive. Activities included rolling a beeswax candle, apple juicing and playing 'I Spy' in the orchard. Sponsorship was received from The Ernest Cook Trust, plus gifts in kind from Tesco and ICI paints.

INSC began pre-school nature play activity sessions for children between the ages of three and four-years and nine months.

August   The ever-popular volunteers' lunch, followed by the sixth Iver Awards' ceremony, was attended by its largest number to date.

October   Iver again helped organise Apple Day at Home Cottage Farm, this year, with sponsorship from Pinewood Studios and South Bucks District Council.

December   The Study Centre's staff and volunteers produced and took part in a live, outdoor Nativity in our meadow and gardens. We had a real donkey for Mary's appearance and again, a real baby. The event was sponsored by the Lonzo Group.

2004

June   Masterfoods (Twixels) supported INSC by coming for a team building day, during which they cleaned the large pond and repaired the wooden bridge spanning it.

A seashore area was landscaped and built at one end of the Centre's large pond using aggregates donated by The Clancy Group, Harefield.

Iver held a 'Senior Moments Week' for the over fifties, offering a different activity every day, such as flower arranging, pottery and stained-glass making.

September   With money from the Lottery's Awards for All, INSC commenced fortnightly Sunday afternoons Art in Nature for Children classes.

October   The first of Barclays quiz nights, in aid of INSC, was held at the Battle of Britain Club, RAF Uxbridge.

Despite atrocious weather, more people than

ever attended Apple Day at Home Cottage Farm, Iver Heath.

2005

Being the sixtieth anniversary of the ending of WWII, the Study Centre, having secured funding from the Lottery's Home Front Recall, created an exhibition entitled 'Dig for Victory' which depicted the Home Front. We also offered a series of events throughout its run.

April   INSC launched the 'Dig for Victory' exhibition, with additional sponsorship from The Clancy Group, Harefield.

May   On 7 May, the eve of VE Day, with guests, staff and volunteers, all dressed in 1940's styles, INSC held an 'In the Mood' fundraising dinner, with dancing afterwards, to the music of The Perry Parsons Big Band. Volunteers Hazel Hook and Kareth Paterson brilliantly organised the logistics of cooking and feeding 105 people a three-course meal. As a result of the generosity of many volunteers and several companies, including John Guest Ltd, Pentax, Lindt and Kall Kwik, the Centre received many gifts to use for raffle prizes.

June   To celebrate the year of Her Majesty the Queen's eightieth birthday, Iver sent a gigantic birthday wishes 'card', with a personal message and photograph from many of the dozens of people who use Iver Nature Study Centre.

July · INSC hosted a Veterans' Awareness Day which was attended by 120 people who had lived through the war years. Our guest of honour was Raymond Baxter OBE, former Spitfire pilot and television presenter. Added sponsorship was received from The Fassnidge Trust.

Timberland chose INSC for their team-building day and started clearing a site for a project due to be launched in the autumn.

GlaxoSmithKline (GSK) plc supported us by holding their team building day at the Centre.

The INSC Horticultural Therapy group held another successful flower show.

The Hillingdon Branch of the Parkinson's Disease Society held their twenty-first anniversary party at INSC, with TV presenter Bob Holness as guest of honour, making a welcome return.

August · The 'I'm Bored' week of children's activities, all related to the Home Front during WWII, was sponsored by Barclays Bank.

The Centre hosted a visit from a small group of children in the care of the Chernobyl Children's Lifeline group.

INSC celebrated VJ (Victory in Japan) Day by holding a street party for children. After playing 1940's games, such as quoits, skipping, marbles and hopscotch, they sat down to a WWII lunch. This consisted of spam, corned beef, cheese and jam sandwiches plus plain crisps, followed by ice cream, jelly and carrot buns, all of which the children thoroughly enjoyed.

September   Fifty-eight people attended the annual volunteers' lunch and 'Iver Awards' ceremony, sponsored that year by Barclays Bank. Eleven-year– old Joanna Pearson became the youngest winner of the Volunteer of the Year Award which was presented to her by Nicholas Smith, a long-time supporter of the Centre.

The launch of the Environmental Impact Initiative (Phase one), with sponsorship from the B&Q You Can Do It awards and the Ernest Cook Trust.

2006

May   The start of basic skills taster sessions in gardening and/or carpentry. Dean, a student, became the first candidate to undertake this project. Under the guidance of Geoff Thomas, he made a nest box. He also learned about timber, different wood textures, the use of hand tools and how to make different wood joints.

June   Anadarko sponsored 'The Iver Experience'. Approximately eight hundred children from ten schools within the London Borough of Hillingdon visited the Centre to learn about the links between food and health, the values of recycling, conservation and the link between the environment and our everyday lives.

September When we were told our INSC birthday 'card' to Her Majesty was one of the many hundreds from around the globe on display, Kareth and I visited The Queen's Gallery, Buckingham Palace to view it and the others on display. Ours, the largest by far, was in pride of place in the first gallery.

     I, as Centre Manager, together with young volunteers Daniella Goble, Joanna and Ben Pearson took part in the 'Fundrun', organised by the Lions Club of Maidenhead, and raised £120 for INSC after completing forty laps of the running track.

2007

January The Mayor of Hillingdon, Councillor David

Routledge, BME, launched our Sponsor a Week at INSC and gave the initial £500 as a personal donation. The volunteer team then clubbed together and contributed £500 the following week.

March   INSC received money from the Big Lottery Fund to expand the Horticultural Therapy classroom. Stu McLennan, the Centre's horticultural therapist, was quoted as saying: 'speaking for myself, I can certainly see the benefit of gardening helping to promote a calm life and boost self-confidence and that is what we are all about.'

October   Loki, a fourteen-year-old pupil at the Autistic Resources Base, came weekly with David, his carer, to work at the Centre. After asking his friends and family to donate prizes for a raffle, he then sold tickets at Apple Day, raising £100 for INSC.

The Chimes shopping centre in Uxbridge sponsored two school visits to the Centre during Apple Week.

ELEVEN

COMPANIES, FIRMS AND GROUPS WHICH SUPPORTED IVER NATURE STUDY CENTRE

Had it not been for the many companies, firms and groups which sponsored, supported or donated gifts in kind, Iver Nature Study Centre could never have offered the wonderful variety of activities and 'Experiences' we put on over the years. These included:

A & C Black Publishers Ltd
Altro Floors Ltd, Hertfordshire
Anadarko Petroleum
Antonia Spowers Design
Arthur Sanderson & Sons Ltd, Uxbridge
B&Q You Can Do It awards
B.T. Smith, Uxbridge

BAA plc Heathrow
Barclays Bank, Uxbridge
BT Countryside for All
Buckinghamshire County Council
Counter Production Ltd, Hazlemere
Countryside Commission
Dillon Booksellers
Dorling Kindersley Ltd
East Building & Timber Supplies PLC, Amersham
EMI Music Services (UK)
Ernest Cook Trust
Fassnidge Memorial Trust, Uxbridge
Frederick Warne & Co. Ltd (publishers)
Glaxo Wellcome UK Ltd
GlaxoSmithKline plc
Graffito Books Ltd
Grassy Meadows Day Centre, Hayes
Grisewood and Dempsey Ltd
Groundwork South
Groundwork Thames Valley
Grundon Waste Management Ltd, Colnbrook
HarperCollins Publishers Ltd
Hasbro (UK) Ltd
Heckmondwike FB Ltd
Hillingdon Parkinson's Disease Society
Hillingdon Primary Care Trust (initially sponsored the Horticultural Therapy programme)
Hitachi Ltd, Uxbridge
ICI Paints Ltd
Iver Garden Centre
Iver Heath Women's Institute

J. Sainsbury plc, Uxbridge

Jardinerie Ltd, High Wycombe

John Guest Ltd, Uxbridge

John Randall MP

Ladybird Books

Legoland Windsor Park Ltd

Lincoln Financial Services, Uxbridge

Lloyds Bank, Uxbridge

Lonzo Group UK Ltd

Lord's Taveners

M & M Timber (Log Cabins) Ltd

Martin-Baker Aircraft Co. Ltd

Masterfoods (part of Mars Inc.)

Maxiprint Ltd

Mitchell Beazley Publishers Ltd

NASA, Washington DC

National Grid Co. plc, Coventry

National Grid Co. plc

National Grid plc

Nestlé UK, Hayes

Netlon, TDP Ltd

Old Hall Plants, Beccles, Suffolk

Pinewood Studios Ltd, Iver Heath

Pitman Moore Europe

Plasto Bambola UK Ltd

Reed International

Royal Bank of Scotland

Royal Botanical Gardens, Kew

Royal Society for the Protection of Birds (RSPB)

Sacla UK Ltd

South Bucks District Council
Southern Electric plc
Tesco plc, Slough
Tesco plc, Uxbridge
The Big Lottery Fund
The Chimes shopping centre, Uxbridge
The Clancy Group plc, Harefield
The Esmee Fairbairn Charitable Trust
The Gulbenkian Foundation
The Lottery – Awards for All
The Lottery for Home Front Recall
The Platinum Trust
The Point of Sale Centre Ltd
Timberland
Trimite Paints Ltd, Uxbridge
Tropical Plant Displays
Usbourne Publishing Ltd
Vesutor, Sussex
Waddingtons Ltd
Waterstones Booksellers Ltd
WH Smith PLC
Wimtec Environmental, Iver Heath
Wolf Power Tools Ltd
Xerox (UK) Ltd, Uxbridge

Our Millennium Calendar Sponsors:
Glaxo Wellcome UK Ltd, Uxbridge
Grundon Waste Ltd, Colnbrook
Hampshire Woodlands Ltd, Alton
Hasbro UK Ltd, Uxbridge

Milbury Care Services (local regional office, Henley)
National Grid Company, Coventry
New Pro Foundries Ltd, West Drayton
Prontaprint plc, Uxbridge
'The Blunt sisters'
The Clancy Group plc, Harefield
United Biscuits UK Ltd, West Drayton
Xerox (UK) Ltd

Two gentlemen I would like to especially mention are Norman Grundon of Grundon Waste Management Ltd, Colnbrook and Dermot Clancy of The Clancy Group plc, Harefield who were exceedingly supportive of the Centre. Whenever I asked either for a project donation, they always came up trumps. One famous 'incident' was when I emailed Dermot, asking him for help with a project, I wrote 'this will be the last time I ask you for money', to which he replied, in one word, 'liar!' I really laughed and, of course, he was quite right!

ACKNOWLEDGEMENTS

I am indebted to my friend and former volunteer Kareth Paterson for her editing prowess. I thank her for the hours she gave to support this project; exactly the same attitude as she gave throughout her years as a volunteer.

Thanks must also go to Clyde Jeavons for beginning the process of editing, until I realised I needed the help of Kareth, who was a mine of information, had kept her diaries and was able to advise me of the snippets I had forgotten.

I would also like to thank Pat Garrard for her constructive suggestions and comments and appreciate her spending time to assist with the final editing process.

Last but not least, thank you to the many volunteers and those who gave me their honest opinions about their time at Iver Nature Study Centre.

Without everyone's help and dedication, this book would not have been written.

Sally Munn
2021